T0330322

MOOMIN MANAGEMENT
Redefining Generosity

Paul Savage and Janne Tienari

BRISTOL
UNIVERSITY
PRESS

First published in Great Britain in 2024 by

Bristol University Press
University of Bristol
1–9 Old Park Hill
Bristol
BS2 8BB
UK
t: +44 (0)117 374 6645
e: bup-info@bristol.ac.uk

Details of international sales and distribution partners are available at bristoluniversitypress.co.uk

© Bristol University Press 2024

British Library Cataloguing in Publication Data
A catalogue record for this book is available from the British Library

ISBN 978-1-5292-4017-7 hardcover
ISBN 978-1-5292-4018-4 paperback
ISBN 978-1-5292-4019-1 ePub
ISBN 978-1-5292-4020-7 ePdf

Cover design: Andy Ward
Front cover image: © Moomin Characters™
Bristol University Press uses environmentally responsible print partners.
Printed and bound in Great Britain by CPI Group (UK) Ltd, Croydon, CR0 4YY

FSC
www.fsc.org
MIX
Paper | Supporting
responsible forestry
FSC® C013604

Contents

List of Figures

1

The Moomin Way

"I have some good news and some bad news," Chief Executive Officer (CEO) Roleff Kråkström began, as he opened the Moomin Characters Ltd monthly meeting during another surge of the COVID-19 pandemic. "I'll begin with the bad. We are unfortunately forced to postpone the big party that we have every year."

This was bad news because parties are a key fabric of the Moomin organization. Parties serve as one means of retaining its sense of common purpose and togetherness. They are a fundamentally important part of the Moomin philosophy.

"The good news is that our performance is the best ever," Roleff continued. He presented the revenues, profits, and balance sheet, and asked: "Does anyone have questions or comments about the figures?" After a moment's silence, he added: "I do. This is amazing! You are all doing a fantastic job! When things are not going so well in the market and in society, Moomin continues to perform. In tough times people go back to what gives them comfort."

Performing well has become customary for Moomin. The business has been growing profitably and expanding worldwide. Moomin Characters Ltd, the company that is responsible for Moomin copyright supervision, is at its core. Giving comfort to people has turned it into a business with a global annual retail value of close to a billion euros. Moomin has developed into a dynamic ecosystem of companies, which nurture a wealth of strategic partnerships.

Ecosystem as a concept is borrowed from biology to denote a complex weaving of relations and interactions where different actors depend on each other. The term 'business ecosystem' was coined by James F. Moore to depict coevolution and reciprocal strategic logic between companies to stay ahead in a continuous quest for capitalizing on innovations.

We consider Moomin to be a business ecosystem because it is characterized by coevolving capabilities, roles, and support of various organizations and individuals. It is based on a shared vision and mutual benefits. The ecosystem evolves around Moomin Characters, which has a hand in thousands of products across the world and trades in copyright and registered trademarks.

Rights & Brands is also crucial for the Moomin ecosystem. This is a company that deals with all aspects of character representation and branding, from publishing and public relations to licensing. Rights & Brands is the worldwide licensing agent for Moomin Characters. Like Moomin Characters, Rights & Brands has daughter companies and strategic partners in different countries. The Moomin world of art and fantasy is backed by solid business organizations, operations, and professionals.

If you search for 'Moomin' online, you'll be surprised to see the breadth and width of all the stuff that is out there. Moomins seem to be everywhere.

★★★

As characters, Moomins are unique. They are amiable troll creatures with pear-shaped faces who live with their friends in the Moominvalley. The Swedish-speaking Finnish artist and writer Tove Jansson created the first Moomin images and stories in the 1940s and soon expanded into comic strips and animation films. Tove, as she is widely known, was both visually and textually gifted. She was original, energetic, and productive, and she had a bit of business acumen too.

Tove Jansson developed an enduring ability to balance between art and business, something that is characteristic of the Moomin ecosystem today. Tove inspired others and developed a way of sharing ideas and working together. She created characters and stories that stand the test of time. The Moomins continue to excite and engage people of all ages.

We are fascinated by Moomin management. Over the years, a particular way of managing people and business seems to have developed at Moomin. We argue that it is about managing with generosity: taking care of people and showing respect and deference, albeit sometimes with prickly humour. Generosity is based on the widely held conviction in the ecosystem that the Moomins offer more than entertainment for people. They help to make people profoundly happy. They bring people comfort.

Generosity can be found in the original Moomin stories, and it is characteristic of how the Moomin business ecosystem functions. Tove Jansson's Moomin stories are reflected in the business as well as the narrative of this book. They offer allegories to discuss management that is open to difference and that aims to treat people well.

In books, comics, and films, Moomins and their friends endure hardships and overcome challenges. They stay true to their vision of life, which is about equality, respect, friendship, and positive rebellion. No-one is perfect but everyone is accepted. The Moomin philosophy is rooted in love, tolerance, and adventure.

Generosity is at the heart of the Moomin way. In managing the business, it plays out as a determined and persistent approach to act responsibly and sustainably. When the environment and humankind are facing unprecedented challenges, and we are surrounded by sadness and grief, managing with generosity is as timely and relevant as it ever was. Generosity can have different meanings and it can be understood in many ways.

In everyday language, we talk about generous people who are ready to give more to others than would be expected or necessary. We consider generous people charitable and munificent. While kindness is associated with helpfulness and empathy, generosity is about giving something that is thought to be of specific value.

In psychology and related fields, scholars such as Elizabeth W. Dunn and her colleagues have found connections between generosity and happiness. Studies suggest that being generous brings us joy and makes us happier. While generosity emerges from selflessness, it is in fact (and rather selfishly, perhaps) in our own best interest.

Neuroscientists, too, have found evidence that generosity increases happiness. Soyoung Park and her colleagues argue that pledging to being generous is enough to make us happier. The decision to give is crucial and there seems to be a connection between happiness and performing selfless acts.

The effects of what is known as targeted generosity are particularly intriguing. Targeted generosity refers to instances where we (think we) know the effects of our generosity on certain people or issues. The argument is that knowledge about the targets of our generosity gives us (or our brain) extra stimulation. Being strategically generous makes us extra happy. This is what Tristen K. Inagaki and Lauren P. Ross's study on different forms of giving support seems to suggest.

However, it would be naïve to believe that generosity is enacted in organizations only to make us happy. There are many reasonable, and perhaps also unreasonable, motivations behind generosity.

Marketing scholar and business professional Leonard L. Berry suggests that corporate generosity is purposeful, channeled, integrated, and oriented towards results. In 'effectively generous' companies, Berry argues, the relationship between social and financial performance is mutually reinforcing, creating a virtuous circle that benefits not only the company but also employees, customers, and the community.

In organizational settings, generosity is often connected to positivity and associated with specific forms of leadership. In their edited book on positive organizational scholarship, Kim S. Cameron, Jane E. Dutton, and Robert E. Quinn indicate that cultivating generous behaviours can lead to the development of positive reserves, thereby fostering resilience in organizations. Generosity can be a pivotal quality in leading people in good and bad times.

Consultant and facilitator Bruna Martinuzzi, in turn, talks about developing the kind of humility, integrity, and honour in leaders that instills hope and confidence in others. She advises us to become leaders that others want to follow. Such leaders give chances and the benefit of the doubt to others. They give others latitude and permission to make mistakes.

Generosity is sometimes associated with what is known as servant leadership that prioritizes the greater good over personal gain. While some associate generosity with authenticity or being true to oneself and one's guiding principles, others associate it with spirituality and a calling in life.

Considering generosity in the workplace, scholars and consultants tend to treat it as something residing in, and related to, individuals. They associate generosity with giving, helping, supporting, and guiding. They celebrate the virtues of generous leaders who invest time and energy in enabling others to develop and progress.

It also seems that generosity can be understood in terms of the teachings of this or that philosopher, thinker, or guru. Ancient wisdom, reciting what can be interpreted as generosity, can be found pretty much everywhere on earth it seems. It is typically assumed that to be generous to others, we must learn to be generous to ourselves.

However, the wisdom of generous leaders is difficult to pin down. Generous leaders appreciate others and listen to them, that much is clear. They show that they have listened, and act accordingly. They distribute information and share credit. Generous leaders build trust and make others feel that they matter. It seems that the list of virtuous qualities of generous leaders is endless, and generosity can come to mean everything and nothing.

★★★

This book seeks to redefine generosity by offering insights to developing a business that is committed to bringing people comfort. For this, individualistic understandings of generosity do not suffice.

There is a danger of slipping into self-management techniques and mindfulness exercises and losing sight of the context that enables and gives meaning to generosity. Individualistic understandings can also lead to a naïve quest for essential authenticity of supposedly generous leaders.

Further, if generosity is expected to reside in individuals it becomes subject to planning, measuring, and audit. Such rigid and formulaic approaches fail to appreciate how quixotic it is to try to quantify and measure something that, we argue, lies *between* rather than in individuals.

Measuring generosity scores of individuals does not make much sense because generosity never takes place in a vacuum. It emerges and finds meaning in given circumstances and conditions, and it is impossible to carve out and measure on its own. Sometimes it leads to great things, but it can also fail and disappoint, as we see happening at times in the Moomin ecosystem. You cannot put a straitjacket of numbers and control around generosity.

Rather than generosity of individuals, then, this book is about *generosity as management practice*. We develop an understanding of how generosity as a management and organizing principle plays out as recurring activities – practices – in Moomin Characters and its ecosystem. Generosity is the grounding for the Moomin way, as we call it.

While generosity is not altruism or philanthropy, intentionality in generosity is a question we return to throughout the book. Critical entrepreneurship and organization scholars Daniel Hjorth and Robin Holt understand generosity as the action of opening possibility without known ends. However, the point about 'without known ends' is not always so clear-cut, or easy to determine, as we will see. Moomin generosity is very much about opening possibilities, intentionally as well as unintentionally.

Crucially, we view generosity as a relational notion. Getting (or not) the benefit of being recognized as generous, for example, is related to how others view generous acts. Generosity emerges in relations and interaction between people – and between people, spaces, and technologies. Generous management, then, is about creating conditions that enable and give rise to acts of generosity.

Focusing on how generosity gets done, we argue against individualist understandings of management – and against management control that is obsessed with metrics and measurement.

★★★

Monthly meetings that all employees are welcome to attend are an established practice at Moomin Characters. As the COVID-19 pandemic once again tightened its grip, the meeting referred to earlier was held online. After a discussion on results and performance, a bit of rousing news was shared.

"I am stepping down as Creative Director of Moomin Characters," said Sophia Jansson, Tove's niece, and a major shareholder in the company. "My son James Zambra will take over. I feel happy about the handover, but also a little sad."

"It's good to do this when the company is doing so fantastically well. It is all thanks to you great people," Sophia added. "Let's keep this short, because otherwise I'm going to cry. I know a lot of things. When there's a question that no-one else can answer, just call me."

"Sophia is still the head of the Jansson estate and its spokesperson," James Zambra confirmed. "She has so much knowledge and so many stories to tell." Roleff Kråkström agreed: "There is only one person left on this earth who has shared a home and spent a lot of time with Tove and her partner Tuulikki Pietilä." His voice was trembling just a little when he confirmed that this was a "natural new role for Sophia". Roleff, also known as Rolle, is Sophia's husband, and they are close.

Thomas Zambra, James's brother, already had a key role in the organization. At the time, Thomas, known as Tom, worked as Director of Business Development. After the handover from Sophia to James, the generational shift in the Moomin organization was nearing completion.

Even in times of transformation, taking care of Tove Jansson's legacy with pride was not compromised. While the business has been growing and expanding, Moomin is still very much a family business.

When Sophia Jansson announced that she was to step down, it was an emotional moment for all. The handover carried symbolic significance, but it was also characteristic of the atmosphere and ways of working at Moomin Characters. The handover was intimate and warm. It was emotional in a down to earth and humorous way.

Sharing emotions is a big part of how the Moomin organization functions. Often it is about positive and constructive emotions such as happiness, joy, and enthusiasm. Sometimes it is about frustration, sadness, and grief – even anger.

Managing with generosity is about dealing with positive as well as negative emotions. It is grounded in creating and maintaining a space where all organizational members can feel that they are respected and heard. Like in Moominvalley, witty and wild humour brings the necessary edge to keeping life interesting. Tensions and conflicts are a natural part of any community, and people need to be able to let off steam from time to time. A shared sense of humour offers a means for this.

And then there are the parties, something immensely enjoyed by Tove Jansson in her time. Parties spice up relations and interaction in Moominvalley and the current business ecosystem alike. They are a good way to share emotions, celebrate together, and spread joy and happiness. Parties are common practice in and around Moomin Characters. This is why the CEO shared the bad news about the party first, before attending to the great figures and corporate performance.

The postponed big party was to be combined with celebrating Sophia Jansson's birthday a little later. It was to be something special – a spectacle worthy of the Moomin tradition.

★★★

Many books have been written about the Moomins and they have encouraged numerous academic studies. Tove Jansson's original Moomin stories have been meticulously analysed. The life and times of Tove herself has been recalled in books, documentaries, and films. The creator and her creations have received an overwhelming amount of attention. Boel

Westin, a Swedish professor of literature, wrote the authorized biography of Tove Jansson.

Surprisingly enough, this is the first academic treatise on the world of the Moomins from a management perspective. Rather than centring on the magical Moomin art and fantasy world, our focus is on the business side. Of course, the two are closely connected, and there would not be one without the other. We draw inspiration from research on Tove Jansson and her Moomin characters and stories but look at Moomin from a different angle.

This book did not come out of thin air. What you read is based on a unique ethnographic study of the Moomin ecosystem conducted by Paul Savage. With Moomin Characters Ltd as his home base, Paul observed the ecosystem for more than two years, interviewed dozens of people in different organizational positions, and had numerous informal conversations with them. Paul developed close ties with key decision-makers at Moomin and took part in social functions and parties they organized. He accessed a variety of documents, visual images, and videos, including works by Tove Jansson, to complement the materials he generated at Moomin.

Paul is inspired by hermeneutic phenomenology and, drawing on the work of philosopher Paul Ricoeur and others, the idea that understanding a part requires understanding the whole, and vice versa. Together with Janne Tienari, an outsider to Moomin, Paul engaged in a process of discovery. Analysing Moomin played out as a hermeneutic cycle of deepening shared understandings of generosity, not as isolated acts, but entwined with the very essence of existence and experiences in the Moomin ecosystem.

Is this book reality or fiction? Perhaps we need to go beyond this dichotomy to capture the spirit of what we are doing here. Paul is influenced by literary scholar Wolfgang Iser's work on the real, the fictive, and the imaginary. Our book is based on real actions of real people, and the artwork is real too. The fictive is about how we craft a narrative about what they do and why, as reflections of the real. In doing so, we point to an imaginary world, albeit implicitly, as a model for how things could be. So, generosity is real, but it is shaped by the interaction of the fictive and the imaginary.

In this book, we take Moomin Characters as our starting point, expand into the Moomin ecosystem, and elucidate ways of working and managing that have been successful in a wonderfully original way. We redefine generosity as a humane management principle and practice and argue that we all have something to learn from managing with generosity.

As such, the book can be read as critique towards business and management practice that is obsessed with numbers, metrics, and performance – and often ignorant of how to treat people well. By redefining generosity, we wish to send out a message of hope.

★★★

The book is structured so that it offers numerous perspectives on generosity. These complement each other and shed light on its different dimensions and forms.

The next chapter presents a journey into the history of the Moomins and the business they have helped to create. We offer a story that traces the origins of the ideas, inspiration, and philosophy that carry the Moomin business ecosystem. We revisit the past to make sense of the present and possible futures.

This is critical for understanding the Moomin brand, discussed in Chapter 3. We recount the delicate balancing acts in managing a global brand while staying true to its roots. Generosity takes the form of managing with meaning, finding inspiration from Tove Jansson's creations where you start with fear and dilemmas, find bravery in yourself, and end with generosity. For the Moomin business, generosity helps protect Tove's legacy. At the same time, it keeps the ecosystem open and alert to the complexities and uncertainties of the global operating environment.

Chapter 4 is about strategic partnerships with companies and other organizations. It is about coordinating and organizing all the different and often passionate connections people (consumers and customers) have with Moomin (its creators and business decision-makers). Generosity plays out as engaging stakeholders and managing with different stakeholders such as licensees. It is about keeping the magic in a cut-throat entertainment business where passion is easily diluted and where only money seems to matter.

In Chapter 5, we turn our attention to strategy work, and learn how the Moomin legacy is turned into performance and growth by doing strategy in specific ways. It is about downplaying the significance of detailed strategic planning and highlighting shared values and orientation towards exploration and execution. Generosity takes the form of managing with vision and purpose, but it also meets challenges of managing across borders and cultures.

New technologies take centre stage in Chapter 6. Or, more precisely, it is about people and technologies and how they work together in the digitalized world. We highlight new initiatives by the ecosystem where Moomins are featured in mobile games and the like and consider what it means to recreate a two-dimensional world as three-dimensional. As Moomin Characters is expanding its digital footprint and offering, generosity is extended to the virtual sphere.

Chapter 7 takes us back to some eternal people management questions. It deals with managing a resilient organization. Generosity is met with some edge when it faces difficult questions of managing people and their differences. It is about supporting people who are 'broken' and who fight personal challenges in their lives. It is also about shared humour. We recount how managing people with generosity enables taking responsibility in and beyond the organization in conditions of the global economy.

Figure 1.1: Tove Jansson, the creator of Moomin

Source: © Per Olov Jansson

Finally, in Chapter 8, we have a party. After all, partying together is an essential part of the Moomin way. Tove Jansson loved parties, life in the Moominvalley is spiced up by parties, and parties are another reason that makes Moomin so special. We'll let our hair down and enjoy each other's company before we continue our quest to make the world a better place for all.

It is likely that the world is going to be even more uncertain, fast, complex, and tense. Questions of responsibility and sustainability will be increasingly important. Organizations and their people need a clear guiding light for survival and success, and we propose generosity for this purpose.

2

Birth (And Life) of Ideas

In this chapter, we trace the journey from Tove Jansson's creations to a global art-based brand and growing business ecosystem. Moomin business is based on the conviction that taking care of people and showing respect and deference to them is crucial for retaining a resilient organization. This is not coincidental. The way Moomin operates today is based on the legacy of Tove Jansson and those around her.

It is impossible to pin down exactly when the Moomins were first conceived. And why should that matter anyway? The Moomin story goes on – or stories, in the plural. Stories develop and they change form. New stories are created, and old ones fade away. There are many versions of what happened when the Moomins began to travel the world. All storytellers tell their own version in a certain light and from a particular position.

Time plays a role in every story. The linear time structure of stories with a beginning, middle, and end draws from classic Aristotelian ideas. These can be used for retrospection and to draw on the past to make sense of the present and future.

Critical organization scholar David M. Boje alerts us to fluidity in the way different pasts and futures come together in temporal sensemaking of an emergent present. Boje argues that seemingly coherent narratives that are built on retrospective sensemaking serve to control and regulate. There are always alternative stories that we choose not to tell or let be told.

As human beings, we tend to impose a form of chronological order to happenings and events, and forge connections between them. We attempt to see stories unfold in, and over, time. We search for and discover plots that we find appealing. We do this although we know that life is complicated and messy, and not very ordered. It is often only with the benefit of hindsight that the plot emerges and the story finds its intended meaning.

★★★

Our narrative of Moomin involves many important characters – and we are not thinking about the Moomins themselves, but real people who have contributed to their success. We cannot pretend to do justice to all of them. We inescapably valorize some and downplay others. Some we fail to mention at all, not because we have a reason for doing so but because, as human beings, we simplify our storyline when we search for meaning in what we see.

There are protagonists (and antagonists) in every story. There is one person, the protagonist, without whom we would not be telling this story. This person is Tove Jansson, the creator of the Moomins. A lot has been said and written about her over the years, and she has become something of a hero, icon, or cult figure for many. Yet she was firmly against heroes herself.

Tove Jansson was a sculptor's daughter. She was an artist who embodied a rare but powerful combination of skills: she was visually *and* textually gifted. Tove was a talented painter, but also a wizard with words. She was a visual artist, illustrator, and author, with a highly original touch. An early critic praised Tove as an artist with two native languages. These languages were images and words.

In her biography of Tove Jansson, literature scholar Boel Westin describes how the Moomins, and their success, eventually became a millstone for Tove, and how she longed for solitude, space, and escape. Westin gives weight to Tove's achievements as a painter and writer of fiction for adults. Tove was also a cartoonist, muralist, memoirist, and more.

All evidence suggests that Tove Jansson would not enjoy the attention. She would likely be uncomfortable with all the greatness thrust upon her. By all accounts, Tove was modest in the way that strong people tend to be. She was determined and autonomous. She became a celebrity, but she was also a very private person. She seems to have loved her freedom in everything she did.

Tove Jansson enjoyed parties, but she also needed the solitude in her remote little island, Klovharun, in the Pellinge archipelago off the coast of Southern Finland. She seems to have found a balance in life where its various, often very different, elements found their places. Emergently, it seems, without a grand plan.

We are convinced that Tove would find our concern over stories, timelines, and plots a bit boring, if not irritating. "Maybe my passion is nothing special, but at least it's mine," she is quoted as saying. So why all the fuss?

It was Tove Jansson who came up with the idea of the Moomins. Legend has it that she first sketched these characters on the outhouse walls in the Jansson family summer cottage. The prototypes of Moomins are still there and many have travelled from afar to admire them. The Moomin idea was brought to life, and it began to take shape.

Then there was Lars Jansson, also known as Lasse, Tove's brother and Sophia's father. When Tove claimed that she was bored with Moomins and struggled early on with the motivation to keep on drawing and scripting,

Lars was happy to take on responsibilities in the creative work. He imagined and drew and took Tove's creations in new directions and to new places.

Lars provided the crucial input for taking the Moomin characters to explore new horizons. He helped to expand the Moominvalley far beyond its original borders. Those who (should) know say that Lars Jansson was not only creative. If possible, he was an even more private person than his sister. He was described as a modest man, putting himself aside and directing his own brilliance to support the work of his sister.

Other key characters in the Moomin story include Per Olov Jansson, Tove's second brother, and Tuulikki Pietilä, Tove's partner. Sophia Jansson, Roleff Kråkström as well as Thomas and James Zambra, among others, are crucial for understanding the way the Moomin business is run today, so more about them later.

But how to make sense of the history of Moomin? How to craft the story so that it shows the grounding for managing with generosity at Moomin today?

★★★

In their book published in the Finnish language in 2017, journalists Nina Pulkkis and Liisa Vähäkylä embarked upon a quest where they sought to understand what made the Moomins into a world-wide success, artistically and business-wise. These authors covered a lot of ground. There was a documentary film, and the book was based on video-taped interviews that were first plotted into the film. Archival research was done too.

The storyline in Pulkkis and Vähäkylä's book was in some ways simple, but it was also tantalizingly complex and ambiguous. It was simple in the sense that it recounted a story of progress and development from modest beginnings to what has become an expanding global business based on a well-known and evolving brand, numerous strategic partnerships and collaborations, and professional management of licensing rights.

Some key milestones help to put some structure around what has happened over the years. Moomin Characters, the company, was founded already in 1958. It developed into the core of the business. It is the official body responsible for Moomin copyright supervision and it nurtures the creative engine in the Moomins ecosystem. Moomin Characters epitomizes what the fantastic world of Tove Jansson has become and what it might look like in the future.

Rights & Brands is a relatively new creation as it was founded in 2016. This company deals with all aspects of character representation and branding, from publishing and public relations to licensing. Rights & Brands does a lot of other things besides representing Moomin, but it is elementary in providing a buffer to protect the creative engine of the ecosystem.

There is also Moominworld, a theme park located in a small island off the town of Naantali in Southern Finland. This was established by Dennis

Livson in 1993 but is not part of the Moomin ecosystem focused on in this book. Livson obtained permission to create the theme park as he had a pivotal role in putting together the television animation series that helped revive worldwide interest in the Moomins in the early 1990s.

Dennis Livson used his persuasion skills for a long time before he got permission from the Janssons to proceed with the television production in Japan. He negotiated with Japanese partners and worked closely with Tove and Lars Jansson in developing the production, which saw the light of day in 1990.

The Moomins boomed in the early 1990s and Dennis Livson's theme park idea was realized. He first owned 50 per cent of the shares, but after a few months bought the Janssons out of the initiative. Moominworld is an example of the different twists and turns in the history of the Moomins, the consequences of which are visible today.

Moominworld is doing business in the name of Moomin but remains separate from the Jansson family companies and the ecosystem. Moominworld operates under a licence contract. All content and products are submitted to the approval of Moomin Characters and Moominworld pays royalties on all park revenues to them.

Beyond its basic storyline, Nina Pulkkis and Liisa Vähäkylä's book was complex. A huge amount of information – many different voices and a lot of details and anecdotes – were shared with the readers. While the book is a treasure trove of information, the connections between ideas, people, and ways of doing things were sometimes difficult to grasp.

So, we put our academic glasses on. Drawing on Pulkkis and Vähäkylä's book, we highlight next what we think are answers to some of the questions that it left unarticulated. We complement our analysis with insights based on our ethnographic research of the Moomin Characters organization and the Moomin ecosystem. This research, building on close collaboration with key actors at Moomin, is the basis for all the chapters in this book.

Our reading of the history of the Moomins is based on three key themes. The first relates to ways of working, the second to products and audiences, and the third to branding, marketing, and sales. We call these the (1) ebb and flow of inspiration, (2) characters and stories that stand the test of time, and (3) balancing between art and business.

These are not intended to explain everything about Moomin, but to help in making sense of the underpinnings of its success. These themes offer a grounding for everything that we cover in subsequent chapters. They form a story about the birth (and life) of ideas.

The ebb and flow of inspiration

The Moomin story from the 1940s onwards is about inspiration: being inspired and inspiring others. It started with the creativity of Tove Jansson, found more resonance in the teamwork of Tove and Lars Jansson, and gradually blossomed into an inspiring brand.

Crucial to the type of inspiration and creativity that made Moomin what it is today are unique interconnections of visuals and texts. From early on, it was not only about pictures and an appealing visual imagery, nor was it only about stories that inspired children and adults: it was about pictures and text that worked seamlessly together. It was about a creator who could do both, draw and write, and who found others around her who could do the same but with a different twist.

From the outset, Moomin inspiration was about sharing. As a creator of ideas and artifacts, Tove Jansson was not overly possessive of her creations. She was happy to share her genius and she respected the talent of others. As such, the perhaps unavoidable ebb and flow of inspiration that is characteristic of artistic work turned into an advantage for Moomin. There were moments of doubt along the way, of course, but the overall trajectory seems quite clear.

Every artist knows that it is impossible to be creative all the time. The more you force it, the more blocked you tend to become. You procrastinate or fall into despair. However, if you are comfortable with sharing the work, the world looks very different. When you are not inspired, others can be. And vice versa.

This is perhaps where the benefit of hindsight kicks in, but it seems to us that intentionally or unintentionally, ways of working on the Moomin characters and their valley offered useful platforms for creating and developing ideas. The Moomins in all their multiplicity offered something that could expand and grow.

The Moomin concept provided endless opportunities for all sorts of productions and merchandise. Eventually, the cast of characters and their home, first created in the 1940s, worked as a basis for a strong brand, licensing, and a growing online presence.

We suspect that the unique interconnections of visuals and texts, combined with the principle of sharing, are one foundation for the Moomin success story. Eventually, all this transferred well into the digitalizing world. Moomins have found new lives in new forms.

The moomin.com website and the online store that was set up in 2013, and the launch of tovejansson.com in 2021, are examples of embracing opportunities that technologies offer. While most digital developments happened after Tove Jansson passed away in 2001, they were enabled by her ideas, creations, and spirit of openness. As such, the ebb and flow of inspiration that characterizes the Moomin story offers insights into the birth of ideas that continue to resonate with people across the world. Perhaps it also helps to understand why the success of the Moomins has come in waves.

In the early 1950s, Tove Jansson exported her Moomins to the United Kingdom. She reworked her creations that had originally appeared in books to fit the comic strip format. These comic strips set the first international success wave into motion. Comics also helped her experiment with new ways of working that proved to be crucial for subsequent success. Lars Jansson's role was pivotal in the emerging teamwork practice as he soon took responsibility for crafting the strips.

Exporting ideas to the UK also made it necessary to give some thought to management and managing the creative process. It led to outsourcing the administering of copyright questions to expert professionals. Bulls Presstjänst (press services) in Sweden became Tove's agent and a long-time partner.

The first wave of success in the 1950s thus helped sow the seeds for a division of labour between creative artistic (team) work and management practices that support it. Key actors in the Moomin ecosystem acknowledge that they would not be where they are today without the kick-start Bulls gave the Moomins to become a thriving business.

While Moomins continued to interest people over the years, the next major wave of success took place in the early 1990s. Moomins set out to conquer the world again, but this time spearheaded by moving images. Success was enabled by multichannel expansion.

An animated series for television manufactured and produced in Japan was a cornerstone in this second success wave. It crystallized what management of art-based work had become: carrying out tough negotiations with potential partners, further opening-up collaborations, and managing licensing rights. And being mindful of the competition too.

Moomin management prepared itself for the new millennium. Among many other things, success in the 1990s yielded the first ever Moomin 'style guide', which set the directions for how to manage the shapes and forms of visuals and texts. Moomin shops were set up. Moomin management became increasingly professional, and it began to focus increasingly on licensing and brands.

From the mid-2000s onwards, the success of Moomins has been steered by a new generation of decision-makers at Moomin Characters. This is when the importance of design and branding really hit home in nurturing Tove Jansson's legacy. This is also when the licensing business developed into professional brand management.

Technology was harnessed to digitalize the Moomins. Moomin Characters' daughter company All Things Commerce was set up to manage the online store and the moomin.com website. Moomin Characters also began investing in some of their collaborator companies. The Moomin ecosystem began to take shape.

At the same time, the 2000s marked a return to Tove's original artwork (rather than the animations developed later in Japan, for example) in the licensed products. These products were increasingly targeted at adults alongside children. In licensing, boundaries of permissiveness became a strategic question. Deciding on who is allowed to do what, and how, in the name of Moomin is at the core of the business today.

How ways of working at Moomin Characters are managed is an outcome of all these historical developments. However, the birth and life of ideas was not only about inspiration and working with inspiration. The fruits of the artistic labour had to be enduring. Translated into business language: to succeed you not only have to do the right things, but you must have the right products and services.

Characters and stories that stand the test of time

In culture and arts, creative expression in crucial. In so-called creative industries, expression is translated into something people want to buy and consume. If you are not able to excite and engage people in what you do and offer, you are not going to last long. You need characters and stories that stand the test of time.

And that is what our friends in the Moominvalley have proven to be. They convey a powerful message, one that is crucial in today's world which is characterized by violence and sadness.

The Moomins are on the side of those who are small and vulnerable. Everyone is different, and everyone is accepted as they are. As a guiding light in life, this principle does not grow old. It can be discovered and rediscovered time and again in different societal and cultural conditions. The Moominvalley vision of equality and friendship endures. It is a universal vision.

Moomin is also about positive rebellion. Respecting difference comes with some edge. Things do not always play out neatly and the Moomins deal with a variety of hardships and emotions. They struggle but they eventually solve the problems they face. They deal with loneliness and injustices in ways that we can recognize and identify with. We can find ourselves in the Moomins, whether we consider ourselves rebels or something else.

Rebels are part of the story fabric, and they blend into the community. The delicate balancing act between conformity and resistance found in the Moomin stories is characteristic of all societies. The Moomins communicate a universal storyline that takes many forms across the world. The Moomin characters – family and friends – are based on archetypal figures. They are presented on the Moomin website, from which we have adopted and adapted the following descriptions. Their relations and interactions, sometimes arguing and quarrelling but always making up, are key elements of the stories.

The world is full of exciting things to explore. This is the spirit of the Moomintroll who is interested in everything he sees. Collecting rocks and shells is his favourite pastime. Snorkmaiden is Moomintroll's friend and playmate, happy and energetic but with a habit of suddenly changing her mind. Moomintroll and Snorkmaiden bring an interesting dynamic to the Moomin stories. Their relationship is full of mutual affection, but it can also get complicated at times.

Moominpappa is the proud head of the Moomin family. He is boyish and adventurous. He considers himself as an expert in many fields and he tends to get a little philosophical. Moominmamma is the calm and collected mother of the family. She makes sure that home is always a safe and loving place for everyone.

As characters, Moominpappa and Moominmamma are in some ways based on rather traditional gendered family roles, but they are much more than that – and while wearing the pinny, Moominmamma is very much in charge anyway. Their harmonious relationship is the backbone of the Moomin stories.

In his analysis of Tove Jansson's Moomin stories from the viewpoint of family, the well-known linguist Christian M.I.M. Matthiessen argued that Tove provides us with an enlightened understanding of the family that is caring and inclusive. Moomin stories challenge traditional stereotypical conceptions of what is (not) and can (not) be, and what can (not) be done, in families.

The Moomin family has a selection of great friends. The good-natured Sniff is always eager to join in, although he can be a bit cowardly at times. Despite her size, Little My is the exact opposite – brave and fearless, but a little grumpy. Snufkin is the philosopher and musical vagabond, a free spirit. Mymble is Little My's sister and Snufkin's half-sister. Too-ticky knows how to solve problems in a practical way. She is sensible and considered very wise. The friends of Moomin are a varied bunch but together they offer an important backdrop to the stories. Sometimes they take centre stage.

The Moomin family and friends represent different human traits. They live in the Moominhouse in the Moominvalley, which is an idyllic and peaceful place. The Moomins function as a collective. They live in harmony with nature, and they welcome all visitors to their universe. Sometimes their adventures take them far beyond the valley, but they always return home. They meet strangers and befriend them, home and away.

It is not all peace and quiet, of course. Stinky is the Moominvalley's ugly little villain, but nonetheless a friend of the Moomins. The Groke is the terror of everyone. She is mostly heard howling from a distance. The big Groke scares the Moomin family and friends, but she is also considered to give some important zest to life in the valley. Finally, the white, faceless Hattifatteners are silent floating beings that are forever wandering in great herds, not doing much but aiming to reach the horizon.

The Moomin stories and characters have many qualities that continue to be timely and relevant. Theatre critic Susannah Clapp wrote in *The Observer* about 'Tove Jansson's crystalline descriptions of the natural world'. Clapp suggested that the main Moomin adventures are 'startingly catastrophic as places are gripped by ferocious forces, laid waste by storms, floods, and snow'.

Natural disasters are a driving force in the Moomin stories, and the characters resonate to the winds and seas around them. Clapp suggested that Moomin stories include visions that today 'read like warnings of climate change'. The style and tone of the Moomin stories are timeless. According to Susannah Clapp, early Moomin stories managed to avoid all the pitfalls of children's books of the period. They are not anthropomorphic, sentimental, or facetious. 'No moral cosh hangs over them', she noted. 'There is no hero worship, no demonization, no punitive framework. Moomin stories are entertaining but also educational, without forcing the education on the readers.'

These are some of the reasons why the original stories featuring the Moomins, Moominhouse, and Moominvalley have proved to be enduring. The books Tove Jansson created in the 1940s are still read and enjoyed in their uniquely comforting combination of catastrophe and cosiness. Their illustrations continue to look fresh, and the stories still resonate. The comic strips exported to the UK in the 1950s, too, have made several comebacks over the years in different parts of the world.

The opportunities that the Moomins offer seem endless. Tove Jansson had already expanded into theatre by 1949 and the Moomins took to the stage in the Swedish language, both in Finland and Sweden. Moomins first appeared as puppets in television in West Germany in 1959 and a television series was produced in Sweden in 1969. Sweden overall became an important market for the Moomins.

After all, Tove Jansson was a Swedish-speaking Finn. She wrote the Moomin books in Swedish and they were first translated into Finnish in 1952. Swedish came naturally to the Moomins. Their life reflects Tove's own and some characteristically Swedish–Finnish cultural features such as concern for each other's happiness, a strong sense of family, and getting together for big parties with lots of singing.

How about audiences, then? Readers, viewers, consumers, clients? Moomin characters and stories have appealed to children and adults alike from the very beginning. Although Tove Jansson denied that any grand philosophy underlies life in the Moominvalley, people of all ages continue to find meaning in what they read and see.

Everyone can discover the Moomin wisdom for themselves. And there is no one right way to do this. Moomins are malleable enough to enable multiple interpretations and learnings. The Moomins have a solid fan base. Moomin enthusiasts can be found in many parts of the world and being a Moomin fan can be a passionate thing.

We are not sure about the philosophy, though. Perhaps being on the side of those who are small and vulnerable, and following the principle according to which everyone is accepted as they are, was so self-evident to Tove Jansson that she saw nothing special in it.

For others, like us, these form a life philosophy and something we are comfortable in identifying with. The Moomins reflect a particular positive view of the world and of the human and non-human beings that inhabit it. We think the Moomin philosophy is about tolerance and goodness. Others may disagree, of course.

Academic scholars in many fields from literature and art to gender studies have debated the Moomins and their philosophy. Business and management scholars seem to have been less active. No great consensus is likely to be reached about all things Moomin. This is the academic way. It is nice that the Moomins keep scholars busy debating and arguing. After all, that is what they do for a living.

While academic scholars discuss the secret of the Moomins, children and adults continue to find them meaningful. Some find courage in Moomins to face the challenges that life throws their way. Some find the stories relaxing and the pictures soothing. Others just enjoy them, plain and simple.

The fact that they have stood the test of time means that the characters and stories are convincing and exciting enough for many people. This is reflected in how the makers of Moomin have managed to achieve the balance between art and business over the years. They have learned to market and sell their products. All characters from Moominvalley are trademark registered and owned by Moomin Characters Ltd.

Balancing between art and business

Art is art. You do art for its own sake. You create for the sake of art. When art turns into entertainment it enters the realm of business. Rich artists can be considered with suspicion, but they are often envied, nevertheless.

Valuing art purely for the sake of art, independently of any monetary value, is a dictum credited to 18th-century philosopher Immanuel Kant. For him, the purpose of art was to be purposeless, existing for aesthetic pleasure and delight, and resting on its own merits.

Of course, it may not be as simple as that. Art is about acknowledgement, judgement, and opinions. Art that is admired in one context may be condemned in another, and vice versa. Art and politics may become entangled, and art can be used for multiple purposes. Cultural policy and communication scholar Eleonora Belfiore argues that cultural value becomes real when it is acknowledged as such. However, she reminds us that it is subject to negotiation and often antagonistic in nature. It can spur disputes.

For Moomin, balancing between art and business seems to have come naturally, and it has developed from curiosity to co-existence to symbiosis.

Tove Jansson was already curious about the commercial aspects of her creations in the 1940s. This was not exactly typical for artists in Finland back then. Some of her peers criticized Tove for selling her (artist's) soul to the altar of mammon. The powers that be in the Finnish arts world scorned the young and apparently successful up-start woman, and never really acknowledged her during her lifetime.

While it must have been frustrating at times, Tove managed to steer through the jungle of criticism. Her curiosity got the better of those who refused to acknowledge the monetary value of her creations.

Curiosity soon developed into a form of co-existence between artistic creation and commercializing the fruits of the artist's labour. Art and business opportunities began to feed on each other. In 1952, Tove Jansson agreed with the *Evening News* in London to a seven-year contract for the use of Moomin characters in a comic strip. How did she manage to do this? From faraway Finland, next door to the mighty Soviet Union?

One thing led to another, as they do. Elisabeth Portch, an English friend of Tove who lived in Helsinki, translated one of the early Moomin books into English. This caught the attention of Kenneth Green, an English painter and an acquaintance who happened to be visiting Tove. Green took the book to publishers Ernest Benn in London. Two Moomin books were published in the UK, and they sold relatively well.

In the early 1950s, the UK, like Finland, was still recovering from the Second World War. Rationing continued to be a part of people's lives and they longed for happiness and entertainment. The Moomins played one small part in serving their needs. Characters and stories that were recognizable but came with a slightly odd twist offered an escape from the grimness of everyday life.

In January 1952, Tove Jansson received a letter from Associated Newspapers. Their representative Charles Sutton suggested a series of comic strips based on what he saw as a satire of conventional lifestyles of so-called civilized adults. Sutton subsequently visited Tove in Helsinki.

The Finnish capital was bubbling with life as it was preparing for the Olympics that were to be held there that summer. Sutton was a true English gentleman, complete with a bowler hat and umbrella. He enjoyed his visit to Helsinki and loved Tove's company. He was convinced that he had something of value in his hands.

The contract was signed, and Tove Jansson set out to study producing comic strips. In February 1954, she packed her bags and travelled to London. She was given a crash course in creating comics by Associated Newspapers. Among other things, she learned the technique of using speech bubbles in her illustrations.

Charles Sutton suggested a pinafore for Moominmamma – and the mother of the Moomin family has worn one ever since. Moomin cartoons spread across the Commonwealth, and they were eventually also introduced to markets close to home in Sweden and Finland.

However, after a few years things were getting a little boring for the artist. Tove Jansson no longer enjoyed the endless routine of coming up with something publishable. Her brother Lars Jansson came to Tove's rescue. Lars took responsibility for writing and drawing Moomin comic strips until the mid-1970s. Co-existence of art and business was enabled by sharing and teamwork.

★★★

Expanding to what is today referred to as multichannel and multimedia seems to have come naturally to Tove Jansson and those around her. Books became comics but they were also worked into theatre plays and television series.

Moomin merchandise became a business of its own. The posh Stockmann department store in downtown Helsinki developed their own Moomin collection and sold everything from Moomin figurines to kitchen ware, towels, and children's hobby materials in their Moomin Corner in the mid-1950s.

Since that time, iconic Moomin mugs have been manufactured in collaboration with the Finnish ceramics company Arabia, now part of the Fiskars group, a key strategic partner for Moomin. People at Arabia understood early on the value of Moomins as a design concept targeted at adults, and new generations of mugs produced from the late 1980s onwards continue to sell very well. Many mugs with Moomin imagery have turned into coveted collectors' items.

Over the years, then, the co-existence of art and business developed into what seems like a seamless symbiosis. Creating meaningful experiences for people in a multitude of ways continues to guide the management of Tove Jansson's legacy. This is about artistic quality but also business acumen and a keen sense of different consumer markets and their expectations.

Japanese people have always been receptive to the Moomins. There is something in the visual imagery and storylines that seems to resonate with them. Looking at the early visual images of Moomin books one cannot help noticing the Asian, or more specifically Japanese, influence.

The delicate but powerful lines and colours in Tove's work seem to be inspired by traditional Japanese art and masters such as Hokusai in their composition and dynamics. Turning Moomin art into business has blossomed in the Japanese market from the 1960s onwards. Generations of Japanese people have discovered their wonders.

However, the stories and visual imagery of the Moomins continue to appeal to people across cultural and other boundaries. Moomin business has managed to challenge traditional ideas of market segmentation, blending target groups such as children and adults.

There are many aspects to balancing acts between art and business. The Moomins reflect their creator, Tove Jansson. She loved nature and the Moomin stories were ecologically and socially sustainable before the word sustainability had entered our vocabulary.

However, Tove Jansson was also keenly aware of the importance of what is today known as branding. She was careful to live up to her image as the 'gentle, cultivated, enraptured child of nature', as she wrote back to her family in 1963 while in the midst of professional obligations on a trip to Stockholm. At the same time, Tove admitted, she 'was feeling pretty cocky'.

Tove Jansson was an artist and an author, and she had something to be cocky about. As much later recited by books reporter Alison Flood in *The Guardian*, 'Tove Jansson, best known for dreaming up the eccentric, magical world of the Moomins, should have won the Nobel prize for literature, according to Philip Pullman'.

Pullman, the well-known English writer, endorsed Tove's life work and said, according to Flood in *The Guardian*, that Tove 'could convey all the excitement of wonder as well as the reassurance of comfort and familial love'.

Many others are similarly inspired. Finnish writer and philosopher Jukka Laajarinne dived into the lives of the Moomins through existential philosophy. He carved out what Moomin characters and stories can offer for us in figuring out questions related to ourselves and our experiences. Laajarinne portrayed the Moomins as therapeutic.

In their book on friendship, in turn, Mikael Brunila, Vilja Saarinen, and Valter Sandell presented Moomin as a rousing example of radical community spirit. They echoed Mathias Wåg, the Swedish-speaking Finnish author, and discussed how the Moomin do not need an 'ism' to work together. This is one reason why they embody a good life for many in Finland and beyond.

So, Tove Jansson's Moomins live on. Art gives birth to ideas, but business helps them to endure. You need a lot of inspiration and characters and stories that stand the test of time, but there is no business without branding, marketing, and sales.

Most of all, our Moomin story is about the power of generosity that Tove Jansson sparked and that lives on in the business ecosystem. The history of the Moomin also helps to understand the crucial role that the brand plays in the ecosystem today.

★★★

While the Moomin ecosystem balances between art and business, our balancing act as authors of this book is between sympathy and critique. The story we lay out is a positive one, but this does not mean that it is devoid of tensions, fractures, and risks, now and in the future.

We are intrigued by what we see. We wish to convey the happiness and joy that seems to characterize the way people relate to each other at Moomin Characters and its ecosystem. It is also curious to see how this in many ways resembles life in Moominvalley.

Generosity grows out of relations and interactions where people enjoy a sense of meaningfulness. Saying all this, we are mindful of how Tove Jansson in her time and key decision-makers in the Moomin ecosystem today are firmly against heroes. In the end, it is the generous community that matters.

As critical organization and management scholars we realize that there is a potential downside to everything. There are always other stories to be told, as David Boje and many others remind us. Some of the things that we have interpreted in a positive light could, viewed more critically and from another position, perhaps look quite different. And we don't know how the Moomin story will look, and how it will be interpreted, in the future.

Figure 2.1: Tove Jansson and her Moomin family

Source: © Moomin Characters™

Moomin Characters have not tried to intervene in what we write in this book. Facts have been checked, but the interpretations are ours. We have received no monetary compensation from Moomin for writing the book. It turned out to be a labour of love for us.

We embrace the balancing act facing us and challenge our own positive interpretations along the way. After all, openness and constructive critique is an essential part of what we think of as managing with generosity.

3

Branding: Larger than Life

Moomin Characters Ltd CEO Roleff Kråkström told us enthusiastically:

'In contrast to the big players who create products and develop assets, Moomin is not manufactured for entertainment. Moomin is a body of art. This is where Tove Jansson's legacy is crucial. Her reason for creating the Moomins was not to generate massive amounts of cash. Tove processed her relationship with the world, her love, agony, freedom, bravery, inclusiveness, friendship, and tolerance. She addressed all the core values of humanity in her work.'

Today, Moomin is a valuable brand. Moomin Characters operates a copyright and licensing business based on registered trademarks, which is about developing and selling the Moomin brand and protecting it from wrong uses and associations. The management constantly works on positioning Moomin in the market and differentiating it from competitors and other players. Coherence and clarity are crucial in branding and storytelling about the Moomins.

Put simply, a brand is a name, term, design, symbol, or other feature that helps distinguish a product, service, or company from others. Branding, as activities and practices, refers to efforts, conscious and unconscious, or intentional and unintentional, that help make those distinctions.

Proponents take branding for granted and critics scorn it. As the communication scholar Dennis K. Mumby argues, branding is a constitutive feature of organizing in contemporary capitalism. It is ubiquitous and 'hidden in plain sight'. This means that we are advised to be healthily suspicious of everything done in the name of brands – and of how brands start to steer our thinking and behaviour.

In this chapter, the focus is on the Moomin brand as an interface with consumers as clients. The Moomin ecosystem is characterized by managing what we consider to be a universally local brand, while staying true to its roots.

"Tove Jansson expressly stripped Moomin of all references to any political system, religion, country or place in the world," Roleff Kråkström reflected.

"The Moomins have a huge appetite for life, and they live happily in the Moominvalley. They are completely unaware of their creator being a Swedish-speaking Finn."

Yet the Moomin brand has in some ways become larger than life in its Finnish home market. Lisa Allardice, chief books writer for *The Guardian*, likened the Moomin 'hippo creatures' to 'religion' in Finland – somewhat paradoxically, it seems, given Tove Jansson's wish to avoid all things religious in her work.

Peter Marten, writing for finland.fi, a website produced by the Ministry for Foreign Affairs and published by the Finland Promotion Board, preferred to talk about the Moomins as a 'national treasure' and as 'semiofficial national symbols'.

The Moomin seem to be everywhere in Finland. To celebrate its centenary in 2023, for example, the Finnish airline Finnair proudly displayed their Moominous makeover. The Finnair Bluewings magazine, made available again to passengers after the COVID-19 pandemic, declared that Moomintroll and Snorkmaiden could 'now be spotted sharing a hug on the bodies of two A350 aircrafts' flying long-haul routes from Helsinki to destinations such as Tokyo, Bangkok, and Dallas.

There is something iconic about Moomin, at least seen through Finnish eyes. Marketing scholar and consultant Douglas B. Holt introduced the notion of iconic brands and proposed that they encourage us to think differently about ourselves. According to Holt, powerful iconic brands operate at the leading edge of cultural change, and they help us to reconsider accepted ideas. Iconic brands create identity myths and symbolism that help sooth collective anxieties in times of acute change.

Holt suggests that iconic brands are not built through conventional branding strategies that focus on benefits and careful orchestration. Iconic brands take on broader meanings and come to represent specific kinds of stories that we as consumers use to address our identity desires and anxieties.

Douglas Holt's focus is on brands developed in the USA, and on their exceptional capability to move us. We are not sure whether Holt would agree, but we consider Moomin an iconic brand, at least in Finland where it is widely regarded as a compelling symbol of ideas and values that resonate with people. The Moomin brand is constantly evolving, however, bringing people comfort in good times and bad times. It is open for debate how Moomin can help us think differently about ourselves.

And it is not only in Finland where Moomins are known. The universally appealing aspect of the Moomin brand can be seen across the world as Moomins continue to resonate with young and old. It carries the potential for being not only iconic but universal or global. The UK commentators cited previously, as well as the Swedish and Japanese connections, suggest that there is something special about Moomin.

'How the Moomin Made Their Way into the Hearts of Nepalis' was the title of an article by Abhaya Raj Joshi and Michaela von Kügelgen, published in *The Kathmandu Post*. They recited how this 'happy-go-lucky family of bare-feet and long-tailed beings' entered Nepal in the early 2000s with a television series. Its appeal was its simplicity and the depth of its characters, and the Nepali-speaking Moomin series became a hit. 'Twenty-odd years on, fans still continue to look for the Nepali Moomins on platforms such as YouTube and Facebook', Joshi and von Kügelgen conclude.

From Helsinki to Kathmandu, via London, Tokyo, and Stockholm, there is something original and enduring about the Moomins that fosters a sense of generosity. From the perspective of the Moomin brand, generosity takes the form of managing with meaning. It builds on Tove Jansson's stories and imagery and translates these into contemporary business operations. Living the brand real every day is at the heart of the Moomin business.

One aspect of this is treating people as consumers and clients with generosity. When the core of the business is copyright and licensing, however, generosity is constantly put to test. Decision-makers at Moomin Characters are faced with ethical dilemmas where they balance between protecting the brand and allowing people to engage with it in creative and, at times, somewhat dubious ways.

The principle is that the Moomins cannot be used for commercial purposes without consent from Moomin Characters. In practice, setting boundaries around the use of the Moomin brand sometimes leads to awkward situations, misunderstandings, and, perhaps unavoidably, some mishaps and mistakes too.

A brand that is universally local

"Moomins were earlier mainly considered as characters for children. Today adults are increasingly our target group," Sophia Jansson, daughter of Lars Jansson and Chairperson of the board at Moomin Characters, explains. "Moomins inspire people. They solve problems with a positive attitude. Moomin stories are essentially about the most important things in life, for anyone, anywhere, anytime."

The Moomins are consistent with what they were when they were first created, but it is only relatively recently that Moomin has been talked about as a brand. Brands are crucial for most if not all businesses. They operate as interfaces with consumers, customers, and clients.

While the Moomin ecosystem incorporates strategic partnerships with companies and other stakeholders (discussed in Chapter 4), the business is based on relations with consumers. These are the people who enjoy the Moomins and have some sort of connection with them.

People can be demanding and moody, and their behaviour is sometimes difficult to understand, let alone predict. Nevertheless, as clients they need to be treated with respect and served well. Without them, very little else matters.

Translating client needs and expectations into value for the company will always be challenging. That is why it is smart to do everything possible to improve the bargaining position vis-à-vis clients; that is, give the old supply and demand a bit of spin through branding and differentiate products and services from the competition.

The key to the client's heart is the brand – name, design, symbol, logo, you name it. The brand is the space where products and services are recognized and evaluated, and where value is created, if it is created at all. As organization and management scholar Martin Kornberger (2010) argues, brands and branding are transforming our lifestyles – and management. Developing and nurturing an attractive brand or brands is a must for all businesses today.

A crucial issue is to develop capabilities in tracking down client behaviours and to understand what lies behind their preferences and choices. Finding patterns in client behaviour and figuring out what they mean for the business today and tomorrow is inescapable for survival and success. Branding is grounded in continuous market research and analysis.

In consumer business there is an awful lot of information that can be sorted out every day. People leave traces online, and this information is valuable. How the information is interpreted and made use of makes the difference. It is not only clients' purchasing behaviour that matters, but their lifestyles and the role products and services can play in how people live their lives.

Moomin Characters has developed systematic ways to keep tap on consumers and consumer trends. Traffic in online sites is followed and social media are tracked. Data tracking specialists compile statistics for retail and media. The data is combined with information on sales and revenue streams. In collaboration with Rights & Brands, who generate information on strategic partnerships, for example, Moomin Characters have their finger on the pulse.

The Moomins penetrate people's everyday lives. Understanding people's purpose and motivation in life and figuring out how Moomin speaks to these is paramount. With every new generation, new motivations, experiences, and connections arise, and the dynamics of branding must be adjusted accordingly.

"We touch people really, really deeply," Roleff Kråkström continued his reflections on what makes the Moomins special. "You consume entertainment, but you deposit your relationship to art very close to your heart. What we offer is cross-generational, as art is, whereas entertainment is very niched."

"We are proactive in managing the Moomin brand," Sophia Jansson added. "We used to sit behind closed doors and say 'no' quite a lot. Now we are curious about all new ideas. In fact, we are increasingly active in contacting potential partners ourselves. People still have a somewhat restricted view of what Moomin Characters Ltd as a company does."

With these considerations, and placing Moomin outside the sphere of mere entertainment, the building blocks of the Moomin brand begin to take shape. Associating the Moomins with art guides the idea of what they are all about.

Perhaps the Moomins are not for just everyone, but especially for those who appreciate quality and seek a purpose in what they consume. Moomin is not an arty brand in a pompous and exclusive way, but art-based in that it speaks to specific kinds of people.

The most fundamental issue in any business is to know who the client is. Too often it is just assumed, and companies act based on their assumptions. At the same time, decision-makers must have an idea of who is not a client. They must pick and choose those who they want to serve better. Too often, decision-makers assume they know, but wish to please everybody, so they end up pleasing very few.

At Moomin, client focus has been discussed actively for the past 20 years. Distancing itself from expendable cheap products and concentrating on quality merchandise was a conscious choice. "Of course, we have done cheap things too, but I think we regret that," a key actor in the Moomin ecosystem admitted.

Gustav Melin, a long time Bulls (Tove Jansson's Swedish agent since the 1950s) executive and one of the founders of Rights & Brands, told us that about 15 years ago, "Sophia Jansson, a colleague, and I put a lot of Moomin products on the table and asked ourselves, 'Is this the way we want to go with Moomin?' We asked Sophia to take away all the stuff she didn't want to see. We began to change direction."

The question of client focus is crucial for Moomin Characters and its copyright business. Drawing on Tove Jansson's legacy and associating the Moomins with art makes the brand available in specific ways. Moomin clients are diverse, and they can be understood from different perspectives, for example, distinguishing between consumers (this chapter) and strategic partners such as licensees (Chapter 4). At times, these client groups overlap, and they reinforce each other, further complicating brand management.

"The Moominvalley represents Nordic values such as equality, education, safety, and pure nature. As such, they appeal not only to people here in the Nordics and elsewhere in Europe and the UK, but to the growing middle classes in Asian countries," Roleff Kråkström argued. "Moomin stories are about fantasy and adventure, but you can find a bridge to family values and the spirit of rural communities of the past. Moomins offer a roadmap to happiness."

In 2017, an interviewer for the *Singapore Comix* blogspot asked Roleff the following question: 'It sounds like your properties have a very strong hipster appeal. Has there been any backlash?' Roleff replied (we can imagine his wicked smile): 'It might be, but then again, our characters, our brands, and our legacy are what they are. We do not allow ourselves to tweak it to a mass market product. They have to be true to what they are. We do not alter them.'

Hipster or no hipster, greed and the lure of fast money are not for Moomin when the brand is nurtured in this way. Balancing between profit maximization and client needs has always been the fundamental challenge in running a business. It is only with the client that true value is generated. No client, no revenue, no profit. No economic value. This is why clients must be kept happy by offering them the best possible products, services and, most of all, experiences.

At the same time, however, companies usually want to secure the best possible return on investment. There is thus a temptation to go as far as possible in maximizing profits without reaching the tipping point where the client no longer wants to buy. This is where the uniqueness of Moomin again enters the scene. It was not created to be a quick cash grab but something enduring and meaningful.

When the Moomin brand genuinely builds on Tove Jansson's idea(l)s of freedom, bravery, inclusiveness, friendship, and tolerance, maximizing profits in the short-term is not an option if Moomin is to retain its credibility in the eyes of consumers. The Moomin brand promise is clear, and it must be kept. However, there are instances where the temptation of profits can lead one astray.

While we are inclined to see Moomin as the brand, it is important to comprehend how Tove Jansson's creation of the Moominvalley acts as its backdrop. Moominvalley, according to Roleff Kråkström, is a complete composition: "We do not want to change it and we allow no guest stars like Santa Claus in it."

The Moomin brand informs everything that is done in its name: "Moomin is a body of art. As a company we must stay true to its values. This sets us apart from many of the other players. As a small player, we emphasize speed and action in everything we do. The Moomin ecosystem supports our capabilities to act fast."

"In our numerous collaborations, we work with the best people, companies, and other organizations," Moomin Characters Director of Business Development Thomas Zambra pointed out. "Within every generation of professionals, we aim to work with the most prominent and promising artists, illustrators, authors, service providers, and creators. We want to find new voices to keep the Moomin brand alive and dynamic."

"We build to last," Thomas concluded. "We are in business to do good. Whenever at a crossroads, our goal is to choose the long-term over the short-term and the values-driven over the commercial. However, to have the largest positive impact we can, we aim to outgrow the industry every year."

Staying independent and standing outside, and in contrast to, the global entertainment giants frame this search for growth. Tove Jansson famously replied with a firm 'no' in the 1950s when the Walt Disney Corporation wanted to buy exclusive rights to the Moomin name and characters.

Today, Moomin is a worldwide trademark with over 700 licensees that are allowed to use the Moomin brand for a set time, typically 2–3 years, in their products, services, and campaigns. Most of the licensees are based in the Nordic countries and Japan. Around 100 new agreements are signed every year. The Moomin brand is neither something that a marketer dreamed up nor a flash-in-the-pan invention, but something that is grounded in a long history of ideas and creativity. Crucially, these ideas live on in people's experiences with the Moomins, and they do so in remarkably consistent ways. These experiences seem to be very similar across time and space.

As observed by the well-known Canadian writer Sheila Heti in her article in *The New Yorker*, Tove Jansson's 'fans clamored for more of her strange and enthralling fictional worlds'. Heti's story was grounded in the observation that 'most of Jansson's fans arrived by way of the Moomins, a friendly species of her invention – rotund white creatures that look a little like upright hippos'.

Like so many others, Sheila Heti praised Tove Jansson's intelligent intimacy and humour as 'she created a reassuring world with a moral code, and characters with problems much like our own'. Heti argued in *The New Yorker* that 'the Moomins are not so much cute as strangely familiar, as though Jansson happened to look in a new direction and find these tender and serious fellow-creatures, who had been with us all along'.

Madeleine Luckel, born in California and writing for *Vogue* about her travels to experience the Moomins, was equally fascinated. Luckel searched for reasons for the popularity of the Moomins and concluded that 'it has something to do with the books' underlying message'. She visited Helsinki and talked to Finns about the Moomins. Luckel learned that 'the books themselves are often viewed as an allegory for the struggle between good and evil'.

These descriptions of the Moomins show again how they are somehow larger than life. There seems to be a personal experience, epiphany, and engagement with the Moomins that underlie descriptions such as those found in *The New Yorker* and *Vogue*.

Madeleine Luckel wrote about her experience of first engaging with the Moomin books as a 10-year-old in Berkeley, California, when a teacher in a summer camp sewing class read it to the children. 'For years I harbored a nostalgic love and appreciation for the Moomins and their world', she recalled in *Vogue*.

Stories of personal engagement with the Moomins seem to come in two stages. The Moomin books fascinate and thrill the child. The experience can then be rediscovered. As the child becomes an adult, they find meaning in the Moomins and look back and reflect on their childhood experiences.

As Madeleine Luckel put it in *Vogue*: 'I may not have grasped this as a 10-year-old, but the world of the Moomins often offers up an example for how to live a peaceful yet adventurous life. And that, after all, is the type of ideal that causes so many travelers to set out from home.' The adult travel writer embarked upon a journey to her own past, it seems, through the Moomins.

People with very different backgrounds find meaning in the Moomins. In Mark Bosworth's article in the *BBC News Magazine*, Frank Cottrell

Boyce, who scripted the opening ceremony in the 2012 Olympics in London, recalled how he discovered a Moomin book as a 10-year-old in a Liverpool library: 'I lived on this great big housing estate in suburban Liverpool, from a working-class background, and somehow this bohemian, upper middle-class, Finnish lesbian eccentric felt like she was speaking directly to me.'

The connection was immediate. Cottrell Boyce praised the Moomin books as fantastically enriching. According to Bosworth in the *BBC News Magazine*, Cottrell Boyce particularly enjoys the importance they place on small pleasures and the message that 'life is really worth living if we're just nice to each other and make really good coffee, and the pancakes are just right – then nothing else really matters in any substantial way. That's a fantastic message to take home, isn't it?'

The Moomins have many celebrity fans across the world. The Icelandic musician Björk is one of them. Björk wrote and performed the theme tune 'The Comet Song' for the movie *Moomins and the Comet Chase*, released in 2010. She has been a Moomin fan since childhood and has often been seen wearing Moomins' depictions on T-shirts and neckties. Björk's artful eccentricity and talent nicely matches the art-based Moomin brand.

Incidentally, the book that Liverpool-born Frank Cottrell Boyce read as a 10-year-old was *Finn Family Moomintroll*. In this translation to the English language, the Moominvalley was located in Finland. In Mark Bosworth's article in the *BBC News Magazine*, Cottrell Boyce was quoted saying that 'I didn't realise it was set in a real place. I thought she'd made Finland up. Finland was like Narnia, with these incredible characters that were so strange but instantly recognisable because you had met lots of them – noisy Hemulens or neurotic, skinny Fillijonks.'

While the Moomins' universal appeal is based on a sense of being placeless and timeless, the fact that Tove Jansson created her Moomin world in Finland does not seem to spoil this idea. For many, Finland is still a bit of a Narnia, strange and mysterious, and Finns tend to enjoy their reputation as being a bit different anyway.

In a nutshell, the Moomins are universally local. They are instantly recognizable wherever you are located and whenever you discover them. Being good to each other is always a great idea, and comfort is an enduring basis for a brand.

Protecting the brand while letting it blossom

Building on the Moomin brand has many advantages. However, it comes with some challenges too. We hear the word 'protecting' a lot when key decision-makers such as Sophia Jansson, Roleff Kråkström, Thomas Zambra, and James Zambra describe the Moomin brand and how it is managed today.

The vantage point is associating the Moomins with art rather than entertainment. "Tove Jansson crafted a wonderful set of iconic picture books. These are considered fantastic works of art," Roleff Kråkström claimed. "They are displayed at MOMA in New York, in the Tate Gallery in London, and many other key museums and galleries across the world."

There are challenges in balancing between managing a global brand while staying true to its roots. Returning to Tove Jansson's original artwork in the 2000s seems like a stroke of genius. This strategic move enabled Moomin Characters to further sharpen the brand and grow the business. However, in markets such as Japan where the 1990s animations were the main interface with consumers, the strategic reformulation called for a lot of negotiations with stakeholders. As Roleff reflected:

'The artwork from the 1990s animation was a bit of a challenge. Tove's originals are much more valued in the fan communities. These are the real deal. The 90s animation was sort of … uhm … a victim of its time. It was also an entertain-esque projection of Moomin, whereas the originals are clearly anchored in the art scene. They are much, much higher valued among Moomin fans.'

Grounding the Moomin brand on Tove Jansson's original works forms the basis for the brand management today. However, the original books and comic strips vary somewhat in their outlook and messages. This variety is turned into an asset.

Roleff maintained that, "Tove and Lars Jansson's comic strips have a much edgier approach, much more contemporary, they comment on politics, things happening in the world, and so on. And there are tons of these comic strip pictures, so we will not run out of artwork."

The challenge overall is to protect the Moomin brand while letting it blossom. Branding cannot be done alone, and it cannot be kept in-house. There is no way of pretending to be in total control when interacting with consumers. The brand emerges and evolves – becomes (re)constructed and co-created – through interactions and reciprocal relations and negotiations among people. This is why the Moomin brand is vulnerable too.

In addition to journalists and celebrities, fan communities are crucial for letting the Moomin brand blossom. There is, of course, the global Moomin Fan Club orchestrated by Moomin Characters to ensure that more and more people can 'be part of the Moomin family'. Club members are 'the first to hear about Moomin news and special offers" and they "receive early-bird invitations to Moomin events'. They also 'get 10% off their first purchase'.

A lot of activities are also organized through the moomin.fandom.com website. Fandom is the world's largest fan wiki platform, and links to a plethora of official and unofficial fan websites can be found on MoominWiki.

Overall, the Moomin brand is increasingly expanding into the digital sphere. A company called 'All Things Commerce' was set up in 2013 to manage the Moomin online store that sells merchandise all over the world. It also "acts as the Moomin media through which we communicate to our fans all that is new," as one of the key actors in the ecosystem told us. "We began our digital operations with full force. We are active on social media platforms such as Facebook, YouTube, Twitter, Instagram and TikTok. Over a million fans have joined us in our fan club and social media sites."

Ink Tank Media helped initially market the Moomin.com website, which was developed to create a coherent Moomin experience for fans worldwide. The challenge was to create content that would engage old fans and appeal to people who are unfamiliar with Moomin and Tove Jansson.

Ink Tank Media wrote on their website that they

> created a varied editorial schedule of stories, which showcased not just the characters and their author but also the culture, country and society that influenced Tove Jansson's writing. We then promoted the stories on a wide variety of channels and in a wide variety of ways. Moomin now has a great place online for a thriving community of fans, new and old alike.

Online presence opens a wealth of opportunities for spreading the work, sharing, and interacting with consumers. It also complicates brand management as the need for authenticity as perceived by consumers is accentuated with new interactive technologies.

Interaction with consumers is more immediate and intimate than before. As Moomin fan communities move to the digital sphere, interaction with them is a continuous journey and challenge. Moomin Characters follows the developments closely.

★★★

In a workshop on 'Moomin Fans as a Target Group in the Digital Sphere' a few years ago, All Things Commerce Chief Communications Officer Tiina Liukkonen and Moomin Characters Head of Digital Jonas Forth led discussions on differentiating between different fans and fan communities, and on making sense of what characterizes their relations with the Moomins. Several differentiators between fans were identified:

- Are they primarily fans of the Moomins or Tove Jansson? (Creation/ Creator)
- Are they more into Moomin products or Moomin stories and the stories behind them? (Present/Past, Commercial/Non-commercial)

- Are they more interested in new things happening around Moomin or in original content and history? (Present/Past)
- Which interpretation of the Moomin stories do they prefer: the originals, the 1990s TV show, the 2019 *Moominvalley* series, fan art? (Present/Past)
- What is the level of their fandom, how casual or devoted are they as fans?
- Do they work around the subject or are curious for other reasons?

A total of 12 different profiles of Moomin fans were specified. These include collectors and product enthusiasts, different types of Tove Jansson and Moomins fans, and fan artists. Also 'high profile cultural influencers' and journalist and academic fans were identified. This kind of information serves as another basis for managing the Moomin brand and targeting products and services to all key consumer client groups or categories.

Brand promises are constantly tested, and this happens in real time. The Moomin brand promise is about love, freedom, bravery, inclusiveness, friendship, and tolerance. It is about all the core values of humanity that Tove Jansson addressed in her work. Living up to this promise is not exactly easy, and it fails every now and then.

Tove Jansson set the boundaries for the Moomins and for what was later referred to as the Moomin brand. When the Moomins attracted interest and she was bombarded with requests for collaboration, Tove was very particular that the Moomins were not to be associated with politics and religion. She also insisted that the Moomins were not associated with violence or sex.

Breaking a brand promise is probably the worst thing you can do for your business. Exceeding promises, in turn, is the fuel that keeps the engine running. In marketing jargon, the client's willingness to recommend products and services to others is the ultimate test for the brand.

Putting structure around branding is an eternal process. James Zambra, the Creative Director of Moomin Characters, was engaged in developing what he calls the Moomin "artwork onion". This is a layered view of the Moomin artworks.

At the core is Tove Jansson's original Moomin body of art. The second layer contains original Moomin materials that are processed and ready for use in licensing, exhibitions, and other projects. The third layer consists of new materials based closely on the originals: style guides, designs, and brand assets such as typefaces and logos. In the fourth and outermost layer are new interpretations of Moomin such as 3D animation or materials created by other illustrators. All materials are built around the core which remains Tove Jansson's original creations.

Managing the wealth of materials by Tove and Lars Jansson, gathering everything and sorting them out for different possible uses, categorizing them according to seasonal use, campaigns, and more, and digitalizing them is a huge effort. It is another investment in a Moominous future.

★★★

Staying true to the brand in the competitive landscape of character brands, led by giants like Disney, Warner Brothers, Mattel, Pokémon, and others, may be a daunting task. This industry is dominated globally by companies that seem to have a keen sense of what brand authenticity means.

For example, Disney's commitment to family-friendly content and its historical dedication to storytelling and innovation are integral to its authenticity. This is related to Disney's historical relationship with the US Patent and Trademark Office and its capabilities in managing its registered trademarks.

This is a delicate balancing act at times, however, as exemplified by Disney's 2013 trademark application to protect its use of the phrase 'Dia de los Muertos'. This is Spanish for 'Day of the Dead' and an established name for a religious and cultural celebration in Mexico. Disney's move was seen by many as offensive, and it later cancelled the application for use of the phrase in the production of food, beverages, clothes, toys, and other products.

In instances like this, questions arise: Which act is authentically Disney – historical dedication, trademarking non-US religious and cultural festivities, or both? Sometimes protecting the brand feels like an uphill struggle. It is seemingly unclear what exactly was promised, to whom, and why. Interpretations and viewpoints vary, and disputes lead to conflicts that are escalated in the media and especially on social media and other digital spaces.

Moomin Characters management is suddenly sucked into disputes where it must act fast to minimize the damage. The management challenge is to avoid the wrong associations for Moomin.

Some years ago, a former 'boat Moomin' (typically young workers dressed in Moomin costumes who entertain children on the passenger ferries crossing the Baltic Sea) shared her complaints on Twitter (now X). The tweet was about poor treatment of people working as Moomins and it was accompanied by two images posted on social media where Moomin costumes were depicted headless and in disarray. It was the images that were particularly delicate from the viewpoint of protecting the Moomin brand. To put it crudely, keeping Moomin heads intact is crucial in all circumstances.

The company that today owns exclusive rights to Moomins on the ferries reacted to the tweet, and informed Moomin Characters about it. The tweeter was mistaken for a present employee, and she was asked to remove the images from her social media site. However, it turned out that the experiences and images were from the 1990s. Moomin Characters was too quick off the mark to protect the brand and had to explain the misunderstanding in public.

Journalist Piritta Räsänen wrote an article about the incident in the Finnish daily newspaper *Helsingin Sanomat*: 'There is nothing dramatic in this. We only want to retain the magic of the Moomin figures and their appearances for children', Roleff Kråkström explained to *Helsingin Sanomat*. 'The magic in Moomintroll's visit is broken, if he suddenly takes his head off.'

However, the 'boat Moomin' incident exemplifies the problematics of protecting the brand in the mediatized world. Through social media shares and the article in *Helsingin Sanomat*, the Moomin became entangled in exchanges of online commentary where it was associated with excessive copyright protection and bad management.

Readers of *Helsingin Sanomat* eagerly commented on the article online. As tends to be the case in online spaces, and on social media in particular, the commentary was candid, and it corkscrewed in all sorts of directions. One commenter claimed Moomin Characters to be 'well-known for their hyperaggressive protection of the trademark with the excuse of protecting art, which has been forgotten a long time ago as the Moomin business is now everywhere'. It was shared as a fact that Moomin Characters 'does not allow fans to share their drawings of Moomin figures on social media'. This, a commenter complained, 'gets the fans' blood boiling'.

The commentary was extended to the poor treatment of precarious workers and bad people management in companies overall. Moomin Characters received their share of the critical commentary as alleged poor treatment of workers spurred heated viewpoints, eventually having little or nothing to do with Moomin itself. Online commentary encouraged others to join in and to share their own (alleged) experiences, which were predominantly bad.

Once set off, these chains of commentary are impossible to manage. An effort needs to be made nevertheless because all sorts of allegations are thrown in the air and some of them stick with people, gaining truth value in their minds and communities. The challenge that management must meet is related to Moomins being associated with the wrong things, and, in this instance, with bad people management.

Another example of the problematics of protecting the Moomin brand concerns the Finnish lifestyle magazine *Image* and its cover featuring a Moomin character dressed as a Tom of Finland figure. This example unravels a complex weave of associations and events where Moomin became entangled in the politics of sexuality and sexual orientation.

Dressing up the Moomin character as a figure from Tom of Finland and putting it on the cover of the magazine was provocative. Tom of Finland was the pseudonym used by Finnish artist Touko Laaksonen for his stylized and highly masculinized homoerotic art and gay pornographic images. In the decades following the Second World War, Laaksonen became a gay icon worldwide for his work.

The leather gear the Moomin character was wearing and the lash in his hand were recognizable and the associations hard to miss. Moomin Characters reacted as the blended image in the magazine cover was a case of commercial use – and, apparently, misuse – of the registered trademark.

In social media from fans and detractors, there were claims of Moomin Characters doing what Tove Jansson would never do – shut down artistic expression, parody, and free speech. In their defence, Roleff Kråkström explained that, as a children's character, the image was contrary to the intentions of the artist, to our childhood memories, and to copyright.

The Finnish media followed the incident eagerly and eventually *Image* and Moomin Characters came to an agreement. They issued a joint statement where they agreed that the content of the cover was important and that they both defended sexual freedom and diversity. *Image* donated to the Finnish LGBTQI+ rights organization Seta as an act of goodwill and support. Additional prints and online access were ceased.

Yet this was a tricky case of brand management for Moomin Characters. Associating the Moomins with sexuality of any kind is something that it wants to avoid. This is difficult given Tove Jansson's own sexual orientation as a gay woman and the fact that this is sporadically brought up in the media in Finland and elsewhere.

This leaves us with a sense that brand authenticity is, as marketing scholar Jonatan Södergren proposes in his historical review, a dynamic concept that goes beyond a simplistic binary division between genuine and fake. It is also clear that consumers consider both sensory and intellectual aspects when assessing brand authenticity.

It seems that Moomin navigates in difficult terrain in this respect. If they want to be seen as authentic because they have deep symbolic and subcultural meaning, Jonatan Södergren suggests having a bit of uncertainty or ambiguity can be a good thing. However, he adds that for brands that want to show they are authentic through their commitment to social responsibility or even activism, being clear and straightforward is more important.

Interestingly, the article that was connected to the contested cover of *Image* was about the Finnish textile manufacturer Finlayson. While this company was a key strategic partner of Moomin, it also launched a product range featuring images from Tom of Finland. On their website, Finlayson presented both Moomin and Tom of Finland as associated with their product brands.

Finlayson was compatible with the Moomin brand as it is progressive and socially conscious, and this connection further complicated the dispute over the *Image* cover. It elucidated the complexities in protecting the brand today, with myriad connections. There are no absolute winners and losers, and the brand must be managed the next day too.

★★★

Moomin is sometimes used in political and religious disputes that have nothing to do with the characters or the company. When the political battle over abortion right was running high in Poland, an anti-abortion campaigner compared unborn foetuses to Moomins in their social media post.

Moomin Characters reacted immediately when the post was brought to their attention. As covered by Tuukka Tuomasjukka in the Finnish weekly magazine *Suomen Kuvalehti*, Roleff Kråkström was clear in communicating that they do not accept the use of Moomin in politicking. Steering Moomin clear of the wrong associations and associations that are particularly sensitive for people is of uppermost importance for the company.

Finally, there are disputes and conflicts that are related to business decisions taken in the Moomin ecosystem. In Japan, Moomin's collaboration with beauty and health products giant DHC came under scrutiny due to the company chairman's racial slurs. Following heavy criticism from consumers and business partners, Moomin pulled out of the agreed deal with DHC on lip and hand creams featuring Moomin and Little My. The representative of Rights & Brands Japan, which manages the merchandising rights of Moomin characters, publicly apologized for the uncomfortable situation.

It was made clear that Moomin does not tolerate discrimination in any form and that the deal with DHC was discontinued. Shimpei Doi of *The Asahi Shimbun* newspaper in Japan wrote that in the face of 'outrage online' Moomin had issued a statement that they 'conduct a rigorous screening of prospective business partners over human rights issues when it is considering a license agreement'.

Overall, in the contemporary global economy that is open and transparent, brand management can sometimes become a form of crisis management. In the mediatized world, disputes and conflicts come to the attention of consumers sooner or later. They are very difficult to foresee and prepare for, but they must be managed nevertheless.

Managing a global brand in different local circumstances while staying true to its roots can thus take a multitude of forms. The DHC incident in particular leads to broader questions of business ethics that go far beyond protecting the brand. The principle of generosity at Moomin is put to the test in many ways, and this is accentuated by its business model based on collaborations of various kinds.

Branding generously

Companies such as Moomin do branding – and as consumers we do it for them, sometimes unwittingly, as communication scholar Dennis K. Mumby reminds us. When we purchase and read a Moomin book and post about it on our social media, we engage with the brand. When we drink our coffee or tea from a Moomin mug, feeling comfortable, we develop associations and live the brand real.

Douglas Holt's idea of iconic brands is built on their exceptional capabilities to sooth our anxieties and move us. Holt insists that this is not done through conventional branding strategies. Branding is about people, as shared value arises from personal and personalized, unique consumer and client experiences, and these blossom in meaningful relationships. For Moomin, this means having to trust others before seeing what they can do in terms of generating new ideas, developing the Moomin brand, and taking it in new directions.

Branding is about engagement. For Moomin, this means not only involving people in the organization and ecosystem in activities to better understand the client but also engaging existing and potential clients and other stakeholders in co-creating experiences, or the pre-conditions for them.

While maintaining brand authenticity is paramount, companies can exhibit generosity in their interactions with customers and consumers. This can manifest through exclusive content, engagement initiatives, or exceptional customer service. Such acts of generosity can create emotional connections with consumers, fostering brand loyalty.

However, remaining true to the brand does not mean stagnation. Companies can exhibit openness in the form of innovation and adaptation, although this is likely to be met with a variety of consumer reactions. Disney's acquisition of properties like Pixar and Star Wars illustrates how innovation can be used to expand the brand's appeal, while also alienating some loyal fans of the original properties. Branding generously is about managing with meaning.

While engaging with external stakeholders, branding is also targeted at meaning making in the organization and among its members, as organization scholars Dan Kärreman and Anna Rylander point out. There is a connection here to people management at Moomin and we return to this in Chapter 7.

Tove Jansson's legacy blends the reality of who we are in this world with the stories of who we could become. This mixture of reality and fiction is not simply about Moomin as an art-based brand, but about being larger than life in the hearts and minds of people.

As one Moomin customer service employee told us:

'People sometimes see us as Moomins. Not as people but as characters. When we respond to them, we must keep in mind that they don't see any difference between Snorkmaiden and me when I help them with their courier package tracking, or when I answer questions about the origin of a product. I am a Moomin to some of them.'

People's connections with the Moomins can take peculiar forms.

Branding is about storytelling. A good corporate story is compact, interesting, and true. It communicates a purpose. A good story is one where people can find meaning – and one that they want to join and make understandable for themselves.

By all accounts, the people at Moomin have managed to craft a compelling story about who they are, what they do, and why it matters, now and tomorrow. The story is repeated, time and again. And time and again, we noted how employees in the Moomin ecosystem lived the brand by their actions and interactions with others. They seemed comfortable in telling the Moomin story and embodying its brand.

This story and the Moomin brand are about generosity. This means openness, curiosity, and sharing, but it is also about staying true to the origins of the brand and actively managing its boundaries. These are established branding wisdoms, and Moomin Characters Roleff Kråkström was quick to point out: "Being generous is not a communications issue for us. We try to do good things, but we don't do them for the publicity."

Branding generously means not compromising on what the Moominvalley represents, what it is. No new characters are, or will be, introduced and no cross-pollination with entertainment brands can be expected in the Moomin universe. In this sense, the Moomin brand is kept stable and predictable through repeatedly explaining to people what is and is not possible, and why.

Keeping the Moomins intact is one example of the boundaries of branding, as we saw in the 'boat Moomin' incident. It seems to be an eternal challenge. A well-known Finnish actor in the 1960s performed a scene as Moomintroll in which his Moomin head came off and showed the actor's face. It was embarrassing perhaps, and a bit traumatic for young child fans of Moomin, but it also shows why the brand is actively managed. The magic needs to be retained, although drawing boundaries and managing them will always be a tough job.

An online commenter in the 'boat Moomin' incident remembered that Moomins had 'lost their heads' decades ago and that this had been permitted by Tove Jansson. The commenter referred to problems in a theatrical production when the Moomins were first put on stage. As recalled in Nina Pulkkis and Liisa Vähäkylä's book about Moomin, in a performance for children, the Moomins' enormous heads lacked facial expressions and blocked the actors' voices, so the heads were removed midway through the performance and 'the Moomin play started to work'.

"Tove wrote in a fire inspector into the production to come and tell the actors that it was unsafe to have the heads on, so that they could take them off," Kira Schroeder, Producer at Moomin Characters, told us. "It wasn't a surprise to those onstage, but to the audience it was the fire inspector who was to blame." Sometimes the end justified the means, it seems.

So, no brand can be fully 'authentic', everywhere, all the time, and for everyone. For Moomin, being considered larger than life means that someone will always remember, and everyone has an opinion. Connections between the past and present and future events are constantly made. This puts extra pressure on branding generously.

In some cases, this means acknowledging, as Sophia Jansson said, "that we are responsible for Moomin, but we are not the only voice that says what the Moomins mean". Engaging in continuous open dialogue about what Moomin means to different people is a cornerstone in the branding work. Continuing, Sophia sighed and said:

> 'this is hard sometimes. As the rights holder and having lived with Tove, is my version of the Moomins right? Yes and no. Each person decides for themselves, and I am sometimes humbled by what Moomin has become for others, even if it's something I don't see. The question is can I let go of being right?'

Apart from this more existential question, branding Moomin generously is based on treating people as consumers and clients openly and with respect. Discussing consumer communications with a team member, Sophia said: "Remember to start every email with warmth and thanks. Even if it seems they are deliberately trying to irritate you."

Several examples were shared where it was clear that something was wrong on the other end of a phone line, but these mostly ended with agreement. If this was not achievable, the Moomin customer services team was apologetic, as we overheard once: "No. Unfortunately that is not possible. Yes, we are sure. No, you cannot go forward with this. We look forward to the next iteration."

At Moomin, there is a sense of generosity in seeing the consumer as mature enough to handle a kind rejection. There is widespread agreement that relations and interaction with consumers and clients is the basis for retaining the uniqueness of the brand. Discussions on its grounding are common practice at Moomin.

When there is talk of commercialization within Moomin Characters, it is always with the understanding that the person of Tove Jansson is not commercialized – only her art: stories and illustrations.

Moomin fans and brand co-creators come in different shapes and sizes and their motives for engaging with Moomin are manifold. There are, for example, the collectors of Tove Jansson's paintings and of the Fiskars-Arabia mugs, who may or may not resonate with Moomin values or with what Tove stood for. They, too, must be taken into consideration when managing client relations, even if they were more interested in turning a profit than in the Moomin philosophy.

Character brands often have a considerable impact on society and culture, particularly those that attract children and families as consumers. From production and logistics supply chains of toys to the virtues and behaviours found in television programmes or games, the range of activities in this business that affect the environment in general and children in particular can be considerable.

As such, social responsibility initiatives and corporate citizenship not only raise awareness of the brand but position the company in conflict with some of its own practices. This dissonance can be leveraged, as we have seen within Moomin Characters, to reiterate the openness to diversity and the courage to change.

These thoughts turn our attention to the limits of generosity. When everything in our lives is branded, brands become ubiquitous and inescapable. When all our experiences are branded, and we cannot escape engaging with brands, we become vulnerable.

Figure 3.1: The Moominhouse with winter snow

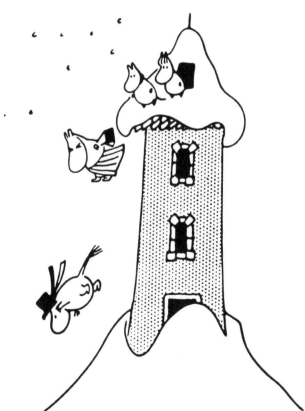

Source: © Moomin Characters™

In his critical studies, organization scholar Mats Alvesson laments what he refers to as the triumph of emptiness in contemporary society. He argues that branding, alongside consumerism and materialism, contributes to a society that is increasingly characterized by grandiosity and empty words.

We suspect that for critical scholars such as Alvesson, branding generously is an oxymoron. If branding is considered inherently suspicious and a source of vulnerability for people, it cannot be remedied.

Overall, being larger than life is a blessing but it also presents challenges. People tend to have a passionate relationship with the Moomins and Moominvalley, and, by extension, with the Moomin brand.

Passion comes to the fore also when we consider the strategic partnerships that Moomin Characters is engaged in. Managing with generosity at the crossroads of passions is fundamentally important for the Moomin ecosystem.

4

Partnerships: Crossroads of Passions

"I enjoy the fact that more and more licensees are using Tove's original artwork, because I think her drawings are unique and wonderful. Businesses are lining up to collaborate with us," Sophia Jansson, Chairperson of the Moomin Characters board, said.

"In the beginning, Tove decided what was a viable Moomin product, then my dad Lars. Now it is me, Roleff, and my sons. I think our values and guidelines have not really changed. Moomin products are an extension of what the Moomins represent, the passion and the philosophy."

Passion, and all the passionate connections and relations people have with Moomin, lead to an urgent need to coordinate and organize activities across time and space. Coordinating and organizing at the crossroads of passions is an integral part of the Moomin business and it has given rise to what we refer to as the Moomin ecosystem.

The sense of passion brings a specific flavour to coordinating the ecosystem. While coordination is commonly understood as the setting up of governance mechanisms and interventions to align interests and activities, at Moomin it seems to be more emergent. Coordination is more about finding common causes and interests than about setting up elaborate systems and monitoring them.

The Moomin ecosystem engages in numerous strategic partnerships that keep the brand alive. Working with companies that share Tove Jansson's vision of life is central to this. Relations with the more than 700 licensees that Moomin has vary in depth and scope. Working with non-profit organizations and engaging in charities and fundraising is a fundamentally important element of the Moomin ecosystem. Moomin stakeholders are a wide and varied group.

Strategic partnerships refer here to Moomin's formalized (through licensing contracts, for example) relationships with other companies. Strategy scholar Robert M. Grant maintained that strategic partnerships help to tap into and utilize strengths of other companies to make both companies stronger in the long run.

This is evident in how Moomin operates. Stakeholder is a wider concept for us, depicting all kinds of people and organizations that feature in Moomin's strategic partnerships. It denotes the fluffy boundaries of business operations. What or who is a stakeholder needs to be determined case by case.

We relate to philosopher and business scholar Edward R. Freeman's work. He is a key figure in stakeholder theory and business ethics. Together with Bidhan L. Parmar and Kirsten Martin, Freeman argues for business models that rest on prioritizing purpose (as well as profits), creating value for stakeholders (as well as shareholders), seeing business as embedded in society (as well as markets), and recognizing people's full humanity (as well as their economic interests).

Ed Freeman and his colleagues advocate integrating business and ethics into a holistic model. They talk about the 'power of and', which is about responsible business without trade-offs, something very much in the Moomin spirit.

In this chapter, we elucidate the Moomin business ecosystem and enter the realm of Moomin Characters' strategic partnerships with companies and other organizations. We pay particular attention to licensees but expand the focus to the numerous stakeholders that have passionate connections with the Moomins and the Moomin brand.

Generosity plays out as engaging stakeholders and managing with different stakeholders. It is about keeping the magic in a business environment that constantly puts pressure on Moomin to do what all others do: maximize their profits and innovate for more profits in the future.

Moomin is something special and it shows in partnering generously. This is a difficult endeavour, however, and it sometimes calls for tough management. At times it is necessary to turn down offers and to disappoint those who are willing to collaborate.

An ecosystem built on passion

Moomin Characters CEO Roleff Kråkström crystallized the principle of collaboration: "Our ethos is difficult to maintain in isolation." The contemporary global economy is interconnected in an endless number of ways. It is fast, complex, ambiguous, and full of tensions. There is always a need for smart collaboration. Choosing who to collaborate with can, however, be a source of anxiety.

A good enough idea for the right purpose at the right time developed with the right collaborators is worth much more than a lonely stroke of genius, wrongly timed. Collaborations need to be coordinated and organized, and this is a major management challenge for Moomin.

The Moomin business ecosystem is built on Tove Jansson's stories, characters, and philosophy. All the key decision-makers we have encountered at Moomin share a passion for these, and they express their passion wholeheartedly and enthusiastically.

For the Jansson family, passion for the Moomins is 'in the DNA'. For others who are not part of the family but have been exposed to the magic and built their own passionate attachment to the Moomins, becoming a part of the ecosystem can be a life-changing experience.

Working for Moomin is a passionate commitment for employees and managers, and this we will explore further in Chapter 7. It is the business relations with passionate attachments and implications within and beyond the boundaries of the ecosystem that are addressed here.

As a business ecosystem, Moomin is a complex weave of relations and interactions where different companies depend on each other. The ecosystem is built on complementary and coevolving capabilities and roles, and it is characterized by mutual benefits and the support that organizations and individuals can offer each other. The shared purpose and vision underlying the Moomin ecosystem is clear. It is about nurturing Tove Jansson's life work and protecting the Moomin brand and letting it blossom.

The ecosystem evolves around Moomin Characters Ltd that is the official copyright holder. All characters from Moominvalley are trademark registered worldwide. Established in 1958, Moomin Characters has grown exponentially in size and scope. The business grew by some 850 per cent in 2004–2019. And it continued to grow under the difficult conditions of the COVID-19 pandemic. Moomin has recently invested in a lot of new initiatives, securing an infrastructure for further growth, and it remains to be seen how its profitability develops in the future.

'Beginning with reviewing requests from small local businesses who wanted to make Moomin dolls and fabrics, we now run a worldwide licensing program', as the Moomin Group onboarding booklet, compiled for the benefit of new employees, puts it.

The purpose of Moomin Characters is to shape and direct the way the Moomin brand is seen and felt, experienced and shared. It seeks to curate Tove Jansson's works in new and meaningful ways. Moomin Characters operates in close collaboration with organizations who wish to manufacture Moomin products or put on Moomin events and exhibitions. It makes sure that the creations are fresh, relevant, and exciting while staying true to Tove's original vision.

Music is an example of this, and a sensitive one because Tove herself was not a music maker, although she did write lyrics for songs. For many Moomin fans, the sound of Moominvalley comes from the Japanese animation of the 1990s. For Finns and Swedes, the voice of Benny Törnroos singing Moomin tunes is particularly amiable. Times change, however. In 2021,

Moomin Characters decided to add to their narrative and visual brand with a deliberate articulation of their sound brand.

In discussion with the multi-talented Lauri Porra, a classical composer, jazz musician, and heavy metal bassist and songwriter, Moomin Characters sought a sound palette for use in animations, exhibitions, theme parks, and more. Lauri Porra's creation, introduced at the Tove Festival in September 2021 with the title 'Seasons in Moominvalley', is a moving piece of music that takes listeners through a story without words.

In response to the piece, immediately after the performance, Sophia Jansson's words were, "I'm speechless. That was …," she paused to catch her breath and find her voice again, "… such a great experience. I need a moment, please." And then, "This musical piece, at the end of this extraordinary day, well, it simply touched me at a level where words are not enough. It went straight to the heart, and perhaps to the core of what is Tove. She addressed our emotions at a level that the intellect cannot understand."

This is a clear example of how new commercial and artistic collaborations with (potential) partners find the right tone through a negotiation of sorts with Tove's legacy. In this case, the sound brand was considered to match the Moomin story and visuals. Other decision-makers at Moomin Characters were equally as impressed as Sophia.

★★★

Moomin Characters has several daughter companies or subsidiaries, and together they are referred to as the Moomin Group. All Things Commerce is its retail and marketing arm. 'Things' that fall within its remit include moomin.com, digital channels, and social media accounts where employees actively engage with fans and consumers daily. Moomin shops – over 20 shops across the world at the time of writing this book – are also under its wing.

All Things Commerce is responsible for sharing the stories and the values of the Moomins with a global fan base, connecting with over 65 million fans annually and selling products to consumers in over 100 countries all around the world.

All Things Content, in turn, is a production company that creates high-quality experiences across a range of platforms, for companies within the Moomin Group and beyond. It offers a range of services from supplying producers, consultants, and moderators to planning and delivering events and exhibitions.

For example, All Things Content devised, planned, and produced the first-ever festival dedicated to Tove Jansson's life and art, held in Stockholm in 2020. One of the reasons for establishing All Things Content in 2020 was to be able to offer Moomin Characters' in-house expertise to other firms and event organizers, to support both educational and commercial projects without direct ties to the Moomin brand.

Förlaget is an independent publishing company focused on publishing and promoting Swedish language literature from Finland, including the work of Tove Jansson. It was founded in 2015 and represents over 100 authors and illustrators.

Förlaget's mission is to increase literary diversity in Finland and beyond. To do that, they balance between books that are likely to have a wide readership and more niche works that are considered important artistically or culturally.

★★★

While not part of what is referred to as the Moomin Group (the four companies previously noted), Rights & Brands is crucial for the Moomin ecosystem. This company is the licensing agent for Moomin Characters, handling over 700 Moomin licensees around the world, ranging from manufacturers and publishers to theme parks, from apps to animations, and to any imaginable Moominous products.

Rights & Brands was set up in 2016 by four founders with equal shares: Moomin Characters, Bulls, Roleff Kråkström, and Bulls executive Gustav Melin. Kråkstöm and Melin were active in the initiative. In the shareholders agreement, they are referred to as the 'founders', with concessions in relation to all other shareholders.

After some months, the Finnish publishing company Otava became a minority shareholder, and Rights & Brands took over business responsibilities of Otava's foreign rights sales and personnel from this function. "We still have a very strong bond with Otava," Roleff Kråkström told us.

Rights & Brands is headquartered in Stockholm, Sweden, and it has local branches in Helsinki and Oslo, the capital of Norway. The company represents also other Nordic brands, artists, and authors apart from Moomin. It is part owner of Rights & Brands Japan as well as Rights & Brands Asia, and it collaborates with international sub agents.

'Our foundation is bringing Nordic stories, brands and rights to a global arena', then CEO Patrick Ullman summarized the Rights & Brands ethos when he commented on Moomin's nomination for 'Best Licensed Brand' in the 2021 Licensing Excellence Awards on the company website. 'Over the last 10–15 years, Moomin Characters have strategically invested in the Moomin brand and our ecosystem, with support and management from Rights & Brands, our Partners and … licensees around the world', Patrick Ullman added. 'We see a huge increase in demand for new alliances and collaborations with Moomin worldwide.'

Roleff Kråkström added that Rights & Brands represents 'literary properties that represent our values. There must be a value proposition in terms of art, design, and they are handcrafted. It is not entertainment. There is demand for such properties anchored in values. We do not want to offer the same things that everyone else does.'

Kobra Agency is the Moomin Group's key design partner. Based in Helsinki, it is a creative agency founded and led by designers. This includes James Zambra who has worked as Creative Director of Moomin Characters. The grandnephew of Tove Jansson, and son of Sophia, James studied graphic design at Aalto University School of Arts, Design and Architecture, a highly recognized programme that prepared him to not only understand Tove's visual work, but also to see how her legacy can develop through the coming decades.

Kobra helps the Moomin Group and ecosystem with their design-related needs, from early concepts to ready materials. Some time ago Moomin Characters bought a share in Kobra.

Gutsy, in turn, is the award-winning production company behind the animated television series *Moominvalley* that first aired in 2019. Gutsy is a team of creators and producers who believe that the world needs content that is funny, clever, gutsy, and, above all, meaningful. Gutsy has been the Moomin Group's key television and film partner, with offices in Helsinki and Bristol. Gutsy has been pivotal in key initiatives in Moomin's engagement with new technologies (discussed in Chapter 6).

Roleff Kråkström summarized the ethos of the ecosystem with a bridge to Tove Jansson's work:

'Moomins is a combination of being brave and respecting your fellow humans and surroundings. Often, freedom and bravery lead to arrogance. But in Tove's stories, the main characters solve the dilemma by being brave and respecting everyone at the same time. It is about doing and solving things together, not about individual superheroes.'

The ownership structure underlying the Moomin Group and ecosystem explains the tight connections and collaboration. Sophia Jansson is the major shareholder in Moomin Characters Ltd. This company has around ten shareholders, including Thomas and James Zambra as well as other members of the Jansson family.

Cross ownership of the other three core companies is predominantly held by Moomin Characters, with minor shareholders within their respective management and expert teams. The ownership structure is built for resilience as the companies rely on one another when needed. This is also a way of managing relationships outside of the core companies, as Moomin Characters occasionally invests in their key partners' businesses, to demonstrate commitment but also to nurture and develop the ecosystem.

Existing research suggests that a meaningful ecosystem is built on a firm understanding of markets and playing fields and a vision of how companies and individuals can complement each other today and tomorrow.

"The Moomin ecosystem is grounded on magnetism between art and business," Roleff concluded. "This magnetism is our fuel." The ecosystem benefits from passionate relationships that various stakeholders have with Moomin.

Sharing the passion in strategic partnerships

'Did you know? Snorkmaiden charms Moomintroll over and over again, even though sometimes they both have crushes on others. Snorkmaiden longs to be rescued, and Moomintroll is happy to help. Their adventures always have a romantic ending. #moominbyarabia #byarabia #moominmug #moomin #moomins #tovejansson #ceramics #tableware #finland #finnishdesign #love.'

This is how Fiskars Group, a global lifestyle company with a unique portfolio of brands, introduced its collaboration and partnership with Moomin on its website a few years ago. Fiskars is Moomin's most important Finland-based strategic partner.

This shows how it is not only the brand that matters for Moomin. People are known by the company they keep. This applies to corporate brands too. In the minds of people, a brand is always connected to other brands. Whether true or not, these connections must be taken seriously. Associations that people make about Moomin and others in developing their lifestyles and making sense of their experiences is a fundamentally strategic question.

The Moomin ecosystem is put into action in partnerships with companies and not-for-profit organizations. This is an integral part of how the Moomin brand is managed and kept vigorous – or, in other words, how it is protected and let to blossom. The sense of passion that is characteristic of the Moomin ecosystem seems to be extended to collaborations with external stakeholders.

While we could talk about brand partnerships, we prefer the term strategic partnership. Many of the relationships that Moomin have with their licensees qualify as 'strategic'. This means that they are relatively long-term and deep, and not only related to branding or co-branding. By 'partnership', in turn, we refer to formal arrangements by Moomin and others to advance their mutual interests, to share risks, and to manage and operate a business where the profits are shared.

Strategic partnering is about capitalizing on associations between brands and finding mutual benefits and, in the case of Moomin and their partners, to do good things, following Tove Jansson's example.

Forming and managing strategic partnerships entails an understanding of the partner's clients. In this sense, in strategic partnerships, Moomin brand management is extended beyond the boundaries of the ecosystem. Of course, Moomin and their partners' clients may overlap. Moomin's strategic corporate partners include companies in different industries and with different products and services.

This is a crucial challenge because there is plenty of research to suggest that a brand should not be extended beyond its identity-relevant core associations. Moomin seems to have embraced just about everything to the extent that we as consumers can wrap our lives inside a Moomin inspired world. What are the limits of this expansion? Can it be truly generous?

Moments of self-doubt are characteristic of managing with generosity. Mistakes are made but Moomin can lean back on core strategic partnerships that are about long-term collaborative relationships based on mutual trust.

★★★

In Finland, Moomin Characters' major strategic partners are sometimes referred to as 'the big three': Fiskars, Martinex, and Finlayson. These companies are committed to responsibility and sustainability in their operations, and their business is close to the everyday life of their customers. Collaboration with Moomin is featured prominently in their corporate communications, and their business seems to be grounded in some of the same principles that Moomin cherishes.

Collaboration with Fiskars Group is well established. The name Fiskars refers to the old ironworks and artisan village located in Southern Finland. The company has strong Finnish roots, but it has engaged in several cross-border acquisitions over the years.

Today, Fiskars' subsidiaries and global brands include Wedgwood, Royal Copenhagen, Waterford, and Gerber. This is in addition to Finnish brands such as Arabia and Iittala. Fiskars' ownership structure is varied, but it includes wealthy Swedish-speaking Finnish families and individuals.

On the Fiskars website, 'moominbyarabia' was presented as one of 'our brands on social media'. Essential to Moomin's partnership with Fiskars is 'the mug'. Fiskars has sold over a million Moomin mugs annually. "When we release a new mug, people go absolutely bonkers," Roleff Kråkström sighed. "And collectors pay ten thousand euros a piece for the rarest mugs. They are very, very sought after. We have hundreds of thousands of collectors around the world who want every mug."

The Fiskars website recited the meaning of the mug:

The wonderful world of Moominvalley has been featured on Arabia products already since the 1950s. The Moomin mugs not only bring joy to the everyday but are cherished treasures coveted by collectors worldwide. Arabia's Moomins are turned from stories to ceramic illustrations by designer Tove Slotte. The designer draws inspiration from Tove Jansson's original illustrations, which she adapts to ceramic shapes.

The mug has become something of an icon. Gustav Melin, one of the founders of Rights & Brands, reflected on its success: "I think it is a combination of things. You have a great mug designed by Kaj Franck, you have Tove Slotte, and you have the Moomins. The mug has proven that it can live forever."

Gustav went on to tell a story about a wonderful surprise: "I rented a cottage that hadn't been renovated. When I opened a cupboard, I saw that they had some 15 Moomin mugs from the early 1990s. Those mugs must have been worth more than the cottage!"

Gustav Melin recalled how Rights & Brands released a limited-edition mug with the slogan 'Keep Sweden Tidy', based on a drawing that Tove and Lars Jansson first did for that organization in the 1970s. He also told us that a licensee in Finland "made a campaign with their product in a Moomin mug, a limited run of mugs, and each mug is now worth thousands of euros." Gustav concluded: "We are all so proud about the mug. We don't need to bring slides and a presentation [to potential clients]. Just the mug will do." Apart from mugs, of course, Moomin features on many other Fiskars products, including tableware and their iconic 'Original Orange-handled Scissors'.

While Moomin Characters is a minority owner in Fiskars, Fiskars itself became a minority owner in Rights & Brands. With shared international growth plans and initiatives, Fiskars Group, Rights & Brands, and Moomin Characters aim to develop new consumer-centric concepts globally. The 'unique' strategic partnership was solidified with this new ownership arrangement in September 2021.

Fiskars communicated that '70 years after Tove Jansson designed the first Moomin dishes together with her mother for the Arabia brand, now owned by Fiskars Group, Fiskars Group and Moomin Characters join forces in an unforeseen way to create more memorable moments together.' In the press release Nathalie Ahlström, CEO of Fiskars Group, said:

This is an outstanding moment for us, as two iconic Finnish design powerhouses join forces to go even more global and tap into new geographies beyond our existing markets. Our shared global ambition, love for Nordic lifestyle and design, as well as our shared values provide an excellent starting point for deepening the collaboration.

Developing new consumer-centric concepts globally in partnership with Fiskars is thus a key strategic initiative for the Moomin ecosystem. Food, beverage, and apparel are some of the other major business categories for Moomin, in addition to homeware.

Martinex is a Finnish family business and a manufacturer and wholesaler of gift items, household goods, textiles, and toys. On the company website, the owner family Muinonen claimed that their 'joint, successful adventure with Moomin Characters has continued since the 1990s'.

Martinex started to work with the Moomin licence in 1991. The first item in the range was the Moominhouse, a toy which remains the company's bestselling Moomin item. The collaboration has been extended from toys to houseware items, textiles, and games. In 2013, Martinex launched its first mobile games under the name Moomin and the Star of Africa.

Martinex exports its products to Sweden and the other Nordic countries, as well as to the United Kingdom and Japan. The company website stated some time ago that there is 'something Moominous' about the motto of their CEO: 'We have always been bravely different. And always will be.' The company proudly declares that over 80 per cent of their products are designed in Finland. Moomin Characters' collaboration with Martinex, too, seems to be characterized by mutual benefits.

The Finnish textile manufacturer Finlayson is another major licensee and strategic partner for Moomin. Finlayson produces bedroom bedding, bathroom and kitchen textiles, and decorations, and all these product ranges feature Moomin characters. We were told on the company website that 'Understanding and loving the home and everyday life more than loving oneself is the base for Finlayson's design philosophy'.

Again, there is a match with Tove Jansson's Moominvalley and a shared passion. Finlayson's history dates to 1820. Some years ago, it was purchased by a group of entrepreneurs who aimed to revive the company's spirit. They emphasized the 'unique bravery and open-mindedness' that had made Finlayson into 'the most loved textile company in Finland'. Social and societal consciousness and sustainability were emphasized as part of the brand.

The Finlayson website said some time ago: 'Oh how we love Tove Jansson's and the Moomins' tolerant, vibrant, and slightly anarchic world. That is why we have a variety of home textiles with all of your favorite Moomin Characters of the Moominvalley. Will you choose the joyful Moomintroll or the mischievous Little My?'

All of the Moomin 'big three' Finland-based strategic partners operate in global consumer businesses. As Moomin licensees, they manufacture products that help make people's lives easier – and spice it up a little. References to 'love' are noteworthy in the companies' rhetoric, and it speaks for the passion in their relationship with Moomin.

Fiskars described its business to be about 'making the everyday extraordinary'. This slogan resonates well with the Moomin brand. Strategic partners share the passion for things that are close to people's hearts and everyday lives. Some of the mundane magic that is characteristic of Moomin is sprinkled on their partners.

★★★

Other major Finland-based partners of Moomin include Muurla Design, which manufactures a range of Moomin products from enamel mugs and bags to candles and glassware. Muurla also has a Moomin for Pets product line.

While Fazer Confectionary makes Moomin chocolates and other candies, the quality children's wear manufacturer Reima suggested that we equip our 'little adventurer for wind and rain. Once back home again, it's time for cosy clothes, a nap and a story – resting in preparation for a new day of discoveries. With these Moomin by Reima outfits, every day is a new, wondrous adventure.'

The number of Moomin licensees increases all the time. An example of an emerging, Finland-based partner for Moomin is the cosmetics company Lumene. Again, we find references to value-based business in how the collaboration is described: 'Rooted in Finnish nature, one of the purest and most unspoiled sanctuaries on earth, Moomins and Lumene share the values of authenticity, honesty and harmony with nature.' Lumene produces lip balms and hand creams with 'the natural, skin-loving MOOMIN X LUMENE formulas'.

Moomin also has unique and single-creation collaborations with clothing and jewellery designers such as Tuomas Merikoski, the goldsmith Lina Simons, and the watchmaker Stepan Sarpaneva. These are more high-end products in terms of availability and price, and they complement the Moomin offering.

"We have exclusive collaborations with companies and entrepreneurs. The legendary brass company, Skultuna of Sweden, made a collection of figurines, priced at 85 euros per item. They were sold out in minutes," Roleff Kråkström told us. "Now they've made remouldings of the figurines and they are selling out again. Every time they make more, they sell out in no time at all."

Of Moomin's over 700 licensees, almost 50 per cent are from the Nordic countries, mostly Finland. In Japan, there are around 260 licensees.

★★★

Japan has been a key market for Moomin since the 1960s. Moomin found a second home in Japan, which has historically accounted for a large share of annual revenues for Moomin Characters, at times up to 40–50 per cent.

The Moomin artwork is appealing to the Japanese and the aesthetics resonate with them. It can also be speculated that Finnish and Japanese societies are similar in the sense that the Second World War left deep scars and urbanization took place relatively late. The Moomins resemble the values of the old village way of life in Japan and Finland. The stories help bridge today's society with the past. "In Japan, the Moomins have been read by three generations who find comfort in re-engaging with the core values," Roleff Kråkström reminded us.

Keiko Morishita is a Japanese journalist who came to Finland because of the Moomin in the mid-1990s – and decided to stay. Morishita is something of an all-round talent. She translates Tove Jansson's Moomin books into Japanese, writes for the Moomin website in Japan, and collaborates with researchers studying Moomin. She works with film productions and television series. Morishita organizes official Moomin tours where her compatriots can enjoy Finnish nature – and all things Moomin, of course.

Keiko Morishita has stressed the Moomins' honesty and ability to live in the moment. In an interview with Anna Muurinen in the Finnish magazine *Seura*, she gave examples of positive associations with Moomin in Japan. Unspoiled nature and freedom were on the top of her list. "'Snufkin is the idol of many Japanese men," Morishita laughed. "They dream of a freer life where they could travel and adventure, like Snufkin does. With adulthood, the reality of life kicks in and men get immersed in their work."'

One key Moomin licensee in Japan is the ceramic ware and kitchen goods manufacturer Yamaka Shoten. This porcelain expert company founded in 1913 started to sell Moomin design tableware in 1998. Their selection includes chopsticks, vacuum bottles, mugs and glass tumblers, spoons, plates, food canisters and storage containers, bowls and dishes, silicon covers, and coasters. Yamaka Shoten has an incredible set of all things Moomin for eating and drinking, catering for Japanese tastes and aesthetics.

Moomin Cafes are originally a Japanese idea and they have been found in Japan since 2003. Benilec operates the cafes in and outside of Japan under licence, in Tokyo and Fukuoka as well as in Hong Kong, Bangkok, and Seoul. 'By visiting a Moomin Cafe, you are partaking in the social element of consuming art and literature', Roleff Kråkström told Hyung-Gu Lynn, the editor of *Asia Pacific Memo* in 2016.

Japan is the home of many other Moomin innovations. In March 2019, Moomin Characters opened the first theme park outside of Finland, in Hanno, near Tokyo. Moomin Monogatari operates the Moominvalley Park in a wooded lakeside setting.

Moomin Monogatari was established with capital from FGI (FinTech Global Incorporated) and other investors. In 2013, it entered into a licensing agreement with Bulls Presstjänst, the worldwide licensing agent for Moomin Characters. Moomin Monogatari was given exclusive rights related to the building and operation of the theme park in Japan. In 2018, Moomin

Monogatari established Rights & Brands Japan to manage all Moomin copyrights in Japan.

The Moominvalley Park attracted over one million visitors in its first year. However, with subsequent surges of the COVID-19 pandemic it was forced to close for periods of time. The Moominvalley Park reopened in December 2021 under the theme of 'well-being'. It was 'reborn as a heartwarming place'.

Moomin Characters also has some very exquisite partners in Japan. "There is the 500 years old Toraya of Japan, making candy in a Japanese way," Roleff Kråkström proudly explained. Their collaboration with Moomin was emerging at the time of writing this book. "Toraya is very, very exclusive. The royal family of Japan, the emperor, had them move from Kyoto to Tokyo, when the latter became the capital of Japan in 1868. The Toraya family had to move because the royals fancied their candy."

In 2020, Toei, the Japanese producer and distributor of entertainment, opened a Moomin Comic Strips Exhibition in the department store Ginza in Matsuya, one of the foremost urban centres in the country. This exhibition included some 280 original comic drawings and sketches, and it featured some Moomin material never shown before in Japan. The exhibition went on a two-year tour in different cities across the country.

This was preceded by the Moomin: The Art and The Story exhibition that opened in the Mori Arts Center Gallery in Roppongi, Tokyo, in April 2019, after which it travelled across Japan. Visitors could experience 'the true wonder of creator Tove Jansson's colorful artwork and thoughtful storytelling via around 500 Moomin exhibits'.

Benjamin Clark, an American professional visiting Japan, wrote a blog in *The Comics Journal* about his experience. Clark was impressed by the Moomin exhibition: 'Jansson worked small, echoing the furtive lines of childhood but exuding a studied charm among the whole over her entire career. Her work is relatable, no matter the age or accomplishments of the viewer.'

The artworks for the exhibition were selected from the Moomin Museum and from Tove Jansson's personal collection. The one and only Moomin Museum in the world can be found in Tampere, Finland. It is advertised as 'an experiential art museum for Moomin fans and art lovers of all ages'. The Moomin Museum includes a collection of Moomin art donated by Tove Jansson to Tampere Art Museum in 1986. It 'brings to life the warmth, wisdom, humor, thrills and spills of Jansson's books and illustrations'.

★★★

While most Moomin licensees are based in Finland and Japan, the United Kingdom was the first export market for Moomin cartoons in the 1950s. The second major Moomin boom there came in the 1990s. "There was the Japanese animation that was broadcast by the BBC from time to time. Around 2015, a lot of the kids who watched that were now in their mid-20s and wanted their own kids to share those memories," Gustav Melin of Rights & Brands told us.

The UK accounts for around 4 per cent of Moomin licensees. In the UK, Moomin has established partnerships with several companies. For example, Cribstar is the 'top online retailer of ethically made and reasonably priced children's clothing'. On Facebook, Cribstar talked some time ago about its collaboration with Moomin: 'This is seriously a match made in heaven!! Tove Jansson was the master of the Scandinavian aesthetic that we try to embody with our minimalistic designs.'

'Oh, what happiness!' the UK-based online store Truffle Shuffle exclaimed when it introduced its 'exclusive range of Moomin clothing and Moomin gifts [that] has all the vibrancy and excitement as the books themselves!' The message was that 'If, like us, you love these incomparable fluffy creatures and their hilarious adventures, you'll feel right at home (in Moominvalley) with our Moomin-marvellous collection of official Moomin T-Shirts, jewellery, and homewares.'

Johanna Stenback, Managing Director of All Things Content, and working with potential licensees and partnerships, said: "Everyone in the Moomin ecosystem has a good understanding; we are taught from the beginning that we should welcome everyone. We will have a meeting with everyone who asks us. Sometimes it's a short meeting and other times longer." Johanna laughed that "all those who have heard Roleff present his gospel have an easier time coming up with something that works for all of us."

This reminds us of the risk of tying the brand too closely to the CEO's persona. This is never advisable, and people at Moomin are aware of this. When preached through a single voice, the 'gospel' is not convincing. Avoiding personification is a strategic issue as new licensees are joining Moomin across the world.

★★★

The USA is an attractive market for Moomin to tackle. *License Global* shared the news in November 2021 that 'King Features Syndicate has announced a new licensing program for the children's property, Moomin, as the brand continues to gain momentum in North America'. For example, King Features introduced new Moomin apparel collections.

"Moomin and its charming characters are known around the world for friendship, love, and adventure and have become a true cultural phenomenon," said Carla Silva, global head of licensing at King Features, according to *License Global*. "We are thrilled to be sharing the Moomin values with consumers in North America through local products and experiences that the whole family can enjoy."

Just Peachy, a California-based clothing and accessories brand, released its line of Moomin-inspired apparel, accessories, and novelty items, including hoodies, sweatshirts, bags, and woven throw blankets. The Ripple Junction apparel line was renewed with Moomin-themed tops, loungewear, joggers, swimsuits, cell phone accessories, and pins.

In February 2023, the Moomin website proudly announced that 'The thrilling, long-awaited news are *finally* in: the Moomin phenomenon lands into the United States! Barnes & Noble is set to make Jansson's literature widely accessible to American audiences, both in stores and online.'

Strategic partnership with Barnes & Noble, the American booksellers, meant that Tove Jansson's iconic children's books from the Moomin series alongside her most popular adult novels were now available for US audiences. Mugs, stationery, and home goods were also available in more than 20 retail locations in the USA, in addition to the online store.

On the Moomin website, James Daunt, CEO of Barnes & Noble, was quoted saying: 'I have long been an admirer of Tove Jansson's creative spirit and the inspiring world she created with the Moomins, stories that still to this day resonate deeply with readers of all ages.' He concluded that 'we at Barnes & Noble couldn't be more pleased to have the opportunity to bring Jansson's work to American audiences.'

★★★

Highlighting the key ethos in Moomin's strategic partnerships, Roleff Kråkström stated that, "We try to push all our activities in a more sustainable direction, all the time." This not only pertains to collaboration with companies, but with other organizations too.

Moomin's strategic partners include not-for-profit organizations such as Oxfam, Unicef, World Wildlife Fund (WWF), Amnesty International, and Red Cross. These globally operating organizations have been vibrant partners for Moomin, and they are committed to the same principles of equality and tolerance.

The point of departure is, as Roleff reminded us, that, "Moomin Characters has formally committed to donating at least 1 per cent of its annual turnover to charitable causes." This is in addition to successful fundraising campaigns that Moomin have helped organize over the years.

For example, in 2017–2021, Moomin raised over a million pounds for Oxfam, a British founded confederation of 21 independent charitable organizations focusing on the alleviation of global poverty. Recently, Moomin teamed up with the Finnish beverage company Olvi in selling bottled spring water in recycled bottles. From every sold bottle, a fixed sum was donated to Oxfam to be used in their projects for accessible clean water across the world.

Moomin was also seminal in raising over one million euros for the John Nurminen Foundation to help save the Baltic Sea from pollution. Over 150 companies and other organizations and an enormous number of individual people joined the initiative. In addition to raising funds, the goal was to encourage children and young people to protect the Baltic Sea. Over 6,000 scouts took part in learning about the Baltic Sea and spreading knowledge about it. Otava Learning, a major Finnish book publisher, donated a 'Save the Baltic Sea' educational package to schools in Finland.

This example shows how, following Tove Jansson, both environmental and social sustainability commitments are central to Moomin, and how these commitments intertwine in the initiatives. Protecting the environment is protecting the people, and vice versa.

During her lifetime, Tove gave permission for her creations to be used by charitable organizations whose work she supported. She allowed the Moomins to be used on materials that would raise awareness of good causes. Tove often contributed brand new artwork for these initiatives, such as the posters she designed for the 'Save the Baltic Sea' campaign and artwork for 'Keep Sweden Tidy', mentioned earlier.

"If Tove would see the state that the Baltic Sea is in today, she would do her best to improve its condition," Sophia Jansson sighed. "The sea is very much present in the Moomin stories. It was also a big part of Tove's life and personality and a great source of inspiration for her. She lived by the sea all her life and spent a lot of time in the archipelago."

Moomin have a strong charitable ethos and there is plenty of evidence to show for the fruits of their labour. Sustainability initiatives with a social focus include collaboration with the WWF, Unicef, Amnesty International, and Red Cross.

Many donations have been made to the WWF over the years, including three euros for each sold Moomin 65th anniversary mug 'Night Sailing', issued in 2010, as well as initiatives in the 'Save the Baltic Sea' campaign.

Initiatives helping children around the world are also timely and relevant. Enhancing children's reading and writing skills is especially treasured by Moomin. As stated by Roleff Kråkström: "We're firmly committed to working with promoting reading and writing as the core asset in carrying our empathy. Without language, you can't imagine peoples' fears, hopes, dreams, your own emotions, so you need to read and to write to be a functioning, empathetic human being. We want people to read and write."

Again, connections to Tove Jansson's work are explicit. The Moomin Group onboarding booklet elaborates on this, introducing the new 'Reading, writing & the Moomins campaign'. This is a continuation of earlier initiatives.

The moomin.com website stated some time ago:

> Through the work of Tove Jansson, we have seen firsthand how powerful a love of reading and writing can be. Not only do these things help us live happier and more fulfilled lives, but they also give us the tools we need to express ourselves and being able to express yourself is one of the most important things in the world: it allows you to communicate your hopes and dreams, relate to others, engage with the big issues of our times, and create change.

Organizations such as Unicef, Red Cross, Oxfam, and the Children and Youth Foundation's Read Hour all agreed to join Moomin in fulfilling the mission in this initiative 'to encourage a Tove Jansson-like curiosity in the next generation and to spark a love of reading and writing in young people all around the world'.

Moomin Characters Ltd was 'on a mission' to support reading and writing and 'we would love for you to join us'. The hashtag #MoominABC materialized in the form of tools and other resources downloadable online as well as a range of products to support reading and writing and Moomin continued to raise funds for their collaborators through product sales of their #MoominABC collection.

There is also the Moomin ABC Exhibition, through which 'a thrilling introduction to the alphabet and a tour of the magical Moominvalley' were offered. Exhibitions were organized in different locations. For example, the exhibition toured the UK in 2022, with the first held at the Eden Project in Cornwall. The latter is a former clay mine crater turned into a 'global garden' with groupings of terrestrial ecosystems or biomes, thus offering a unique, evidently Moominous location to host the Moomins and their valley.

Moomin has also been active in recent years in helping revive indigenous languages that are under threat of becoming extinct. Nanette Forsström, who is Producer at Moomin Characters, told us that "with our project with PEN International, Moomin Characters are having Tove Jansson's book *The Invisible Child* translated into several indigenous languages in Central America and Africa".

Many of these indigenous languages have few native speakers, and this is a way for locals to have literature in their language. The Moomin initiative is not run for commercial gain. It is grounded in recognizing that indigenous languages under threat are as important as other languages.

'Better to light a candle than curse the darkness' is the slogan for Amnesty International. Surprise, surprise, this is not an example of Tove Jansson's immortal wisdom, but an ancient Chinese proverb. Amnesty International teamed up with Moomin Characters to launch a brand-new limited range of products such as canvas bags, beanies, water bottles, matchsticks, candles, sweaters, and T-shirts, with 10 per cent of all proceeds going towards Amnesty's global human rights work.

Moomin figures with candles embody the Amnesty spirit. "These illustrations by Tove Jansson were not only lovely works by a great artist, but also a reflection of the values she held dear: a belief that things can change for the better if we act together," Roleff Kråkström summed up the collaboration.

Some academic researchers who do important work but suffer from precarious working conditions and lack of funding have also benefitted from Moomin generosity. Roleff told us how Moomin began to support a researcher who they felt was doing invaluable research within a group but whose funding was suddenly discontinued by their university.

Moomin first offered "emergency funding", as Roleff called it, and then developed new lines of products relating to the researcher's field with some of their partners. Moomin agreed to lower their royalties if the partners agreed to donate to the research group's funding.

Being generous and doing good is only limited by imagination. Moomin are constantly on the lookout for new business initiatives that enable them to be generous. The new line of products in the researcher's case was something that Moomin had previously avoided.

Roleff got a little metaphorical when he described the solution that they came up with: "Well, we opened the gates to hell, but in a way that suits us and Tove's legacy. What had felt impossible suddenly seemed doable, when viewed in the right light."

While all these examples of collaboration tell a happy story about the Moomin ecosystem and its various strategic partners and partnerships, coordinating and organizing collaborations at the crossroads of passions is not easy. Like Tove Jansson in her time, decision-makers at Moomin Characters experience how difficult it is to be desirable. When everyone wants a piece of the Moomin brand and story, generosity is again put to the test.

Partnering generously

The Moomin ecosystem functions through strategic partnerships. How the ecosystem and partnerships operate relates to, but also differs from, how generosity is commonly understood in business studies. Ecosystems rely on reciprocity, that is, giving and taking. While taking resources from ecosystem partners is obvious, perhaps, giving back may be viewed more suspiciously.

A study by management scholar Muhammed Aftab Alam and his colleagues yet confirmed that companies 'do well by doing good' when they share resources. In fact, the authors argued, companies can bolster their competitive advantage by sharing. One reason for this is simple: generosity tends to smoothen out human relations. This corresponds to the Moomin way.

Strategy expert Claudio Garcia, in turn, proposed that generous ecosystems must be carefully planned to ensure fairness in sharing. They must have a purpose, that is, a clear challenge or opportunity that can better be tackled by an ecosystem than by a single company. They must have flexible boundaries and nurture dynamic networks between participants, based on the premise that human interactions are not random but driven by the perceived quality and reciprocity of a relationship.

Garcia argued for tracking, monitoring, and measuring generosity, and governing it with an elaborate framework. This is where our observations at Moomin begin to diverge with existing research and business advice. Perhaps meticulous monitoring and measuring are needed in ecosystems with hundreds of partners or 'players', as Claudio Garcia called them (somewhat unfortunately for highlighting generosity, we think). Yet, we argue, the spirit of generosity may be lost when it is tamed into a framework that is slavishly followed.

We insist that generosity does not reside in individuals. It plays out between individuals and organizations in relations, actions, and interactions. Creating conditions for generosity to blossom is a key aspect, and it can have sometimes surprising consequences.

Trying to be effectively generous, and consciously looking to reap benefits of generosity, we think, muddles the idea of generosity in management altogether. The essence of what generosity is (and what it can be) is forgotten when it is subject to maximizing short-term profits. At Moomin a degree of emergence and flexibility characterizes how generosity plays out, as seen in Roleff's comment "opening the gates to hell, but in a way that suits us and Tove's legacy", with a new line of products.

While Moomin adds licensees to work with, and more strategic partnerships are developed worldwide, setting the boundaries for collaboration becomes a key management question. Often, decision-makers in the Moomin ecosystem are forced to say 'no' to offers.

Roleff Kråkström told us:

'I have the unfortunate task of telling someone who is very excited about working with us, that we cannot do what they want. We tell them that "unfortunately, we cannot make any commitments, but we are very flattered about your interest". We protect the scarcity of Tove's work, because she has passed away, and there will be no new works of art.'

★★★

How do you partner generously, then? At Moomin, the boundaries for collaboration are set by Tove Jansson's legacy. The form of stakeholder management practised at Moomin is informed by values and a long-term approach.

Generosity plays out in engaging with different stakeholders and managing (with) them. Sometimes collaboration and partnerships kick off very well. Roleff Kråkström spoke at Moomin Day, a meeting of the Moomin Group and their licensing arm, Rights & Brands. He said:

'We have a structure, strategy, and a vision of what we want to do, with whom ideally and we are proactive. Then this company came from nowhere. Very spontaneously, very quickly, we realized that they speak the same language as we do, and they thoroughly get what we want to achieve.'

Roleff continued:

'They are very self-driven, entrepreneurial, and we took a risk, in a way, and gave them a big field and just said, "Go". And it's gone fantastically. In six months, they are a top licensee. They are expanding in new directions. So, we shouldn't lose our tenderness, if you like, or our curiosity, and our willingness to do stuff really quickly sometimes.'

Then there are also licensees whose relationships with the Moomin have been more troublesome. A key actor in the ecosystem sighed:

'Everyone talks about values, but I can think of this one licensee representative who still calls the characters "Moomin Guys" because they aren't interested in them enough to remember the correct name. It's a rather high-end product they sell. They know it works commercially but don't know about Moomin values so much. The people who buy the product might do because of the love or friendship in the stories and brand, but they don't really care.'

Controlling strategic partners, let alone their possible sub-contractors (and their possible sub-contractors and so on), is notoriously difficult. While the stakeholders around Moomin may appear generous, someone, somewhere, may act irresponsibly, breaching their contracts. Generosity can appear hypocritical or fake.

Managing strategic partnerships is a continuous process that can lead in numerous directions. A Japanese Moomin licensee suggested that a well-known social media influencer (and the licensee's collaborator) would do a spectacular Moomin video. They would start with the Moomin costume on and then half-way through the broadcast pop the head off and reveal themselves. The short-term commercial benefits were clear as the video could encourage the influencer's fans to find out more about Moomin characters and engage with them. However, the approvals team at Moomin said 'no'. There were two reasons for this.

First, the locating of Moomin outside of Moominvalley and inside the world of non-fictional entertainment would explicitly give the fictional Moomins' approval and reference to a real individual. This is something that Moomin Characters explicitly wants to avoid because it is not in line with Tove Jansson's original ideas.

Second, the removing of the head and seeing that inside the Moomin is a human being (located in time and place) contradicts the idea that Moomins are timeless and placeless. This is a recurring issue in protecting the brand, as seen in the 'boat Moomin' incident mentioned earlier.

In many ways, balancing between art and business is a constant feature of managing partnerships in the Moomin ecosystem. We observed an interesting exchange of words by Roleff Kråkström and Sophia Jansson within a planning meeting regarding the launch of the new tove.com website, which focuses on the life and work of Tove Jansson, way beyond her Moomin creations. While the encounter shows how the brand is constantly worked on, it also provides an insight into how management is performed at Moomin more generally.

"This website should be like a gallery, a curated exhibition of art, a cultural space for those who want to interact with Tove and her art," Roleff envisioned. "But it should not be driving people to moomin.com. If they want to, they will find it easily enough anyway." Sophia responded: "I don't agree. When I go to the Louvre, I want to go through the gift shop and maybe get a poster or a book. It's not commercializing. It's letting people remember their experience."

Witnessing this disagreement, Moomin Characters employees were encouraged to share their views. As one employee told us later:

'We all know that Rolle and Sophia do not have to agree on everything. No-one forces the other to accept things about which they can have different opinions. We all know that we must be able to defend our views and opinions, too, and Rolle and Sophia will change their minds if we know better.'

Not agreeing on everything and managing to discuss and reconcile different viewpoints and to reach decisions is an integral part of how the Moomin business is run today. It is reflected in the branding, which can never be perfect, and it characterizes all aspects of management at Moomin. It culminates in the collaboration with strategic partners.

Figure 4.1: Moominpappa goes to work

Source: © Moomin Characters™

Retaining the ethos of generosity in the strategic partnerships is a constant challenge for Moomin. The number of licensees is growing and keeping taps on their values base and conduct is essential. The Moomin principle is, as Roleff put it, that "we get our voice heard in each and every collaboration and partnership".

Next, we look into the future and consider how strategy is done in the Moomin ecosystem. We explore the purpose of Moomin and build an understanding on how it is projected ahead and how it impacts upon generosity.

5

Strategy: What's the Purpose?

'We know that there is always more that can be done, so we are always looking into new ways that we can grow our efforts and develop what has come before', the Moomin Group onboarding booklet boldly states.

In life, nothing lasts forever. The same applies to business activities. While taking care of the brand and strategic partnerships today, the Moomin ecosystem engages with the future, or multiple possible futures, and tries to figure out what is likely to happen next. There is a forward-looking and proactive stance in the ecosystem. We refer to this as strategy work, that is activities, practices, and talk that look beyond the horizon. This can also be called strategizing.

The crucial thing in doing strategy is to engage in joint activities that lead to smart choices and decisions; to turn strategic ideas into actions. As Richard Whittington and other 'strategy as practice' scholars have argued, strategy only comes into being when it gets done. This seemingly self-evident fact is often forgotten in traditional takes on strategy focused on analysis and planning.

Working on the future(s) strategically is about purpose, vision, and values. Purpose, or mission, is the reason for existing. Vision is a target state. Values are shared beliefs that offer a framework for actions.

The purpose, or mission, in the Moomin ecosystem is to spread the joy of the Moomin stories and to promote the values they represent globally. The vision of Moomin Characters Ltd at the centre of the ecosystem is to be the number one art-based licensing company in the world.

The question is how to fulfil the purpose and realize the vision, not only today but tomorrow? For Moomin, this is about becoming better and better in creating products and services based on Tove Jansson's art globally in ways that appeal to those who are looking for an alternative to the mainstream entertainment industry.

This leads us to strategy and to making things happen. Figuring out where to allocate resources (and where not) is the classic strategic question, referred to as 'men, money, and materials' by pioneering strategy scholar Alfred D. Chandler, and recounted in numerous studies after him.

In this sense, strategy is about decisions and choices, or making bets on the future. Deciding what not to do is, of course, equally important. However, there is a lot of talk about strategy and some of it is disturbingly ambiguous. According to Henry Mintzberg (1987), another well-known strategy scholar, five basic ways of conceiving strategy prevail. Strategy can refer to a plan, ploy, pattern, position, or perspective.

Mintzberg's heuristic of 5 P's is useful because too often we just assume that we are talking about the same thing when we talk strategy with others. Talking about strategy as if it was a plan is perhaps the most traditional and common way. Therein, strategy takes the form of a carefully crafted set of steps that a firm intends to follow in growing profitably.

For Henry Mintzberg (1994), however, strategy is much more than a plan. Strategy is about synthesizing ideas creatively. Over the years, Mintzberg has consistently argued for rethinking strategy. Planners should not create strategies, he says, but help supply the data. The most successful strategies are visions, not plans.

We draw inspiration from Henry Mintzberg's ideas and analyse Moomin in the spirit of strategy as practice research. We see strategy as a verb, rather than a noun. Strategy work refers to recurring activities, or practices, through which things get done. It also refers to how strategy is talked about. There is no doing without talking.

In this chapter, we trace how strategy is done in the Moomin ecosystem and consider how generosity plays into its strategy work. As the Moomin Group onboarding booklet states, 'we have become a very successful and respected international business, driven by the desire to safeguard Tove Jansson's body of work for generations to come, so that they too can benefit from its profound wisdom'.

Generosity 'for generations to come' takes the form of managing with purpose, vision, and values. However, strategy work aimed at the future will always be a battleground for competing truths. Disputes between different possible forms of generosity add spice to strategy work at Moomin. Strategy stirs emotions and it is heatedly debated at times.

Values as bridges from the past to the future

'What has remained constant from the 1950s is that we are led by our values above all else – values which we derive from the Moomin stories', the Moomin Group onboarding booklet informed us. 'To help guide us as a business, we have distilled these values into three key concepts: 1) Love. 2) Equality. 3) Courage.'

Strategy is about alternative futures and engaging with the unknown. The key point in strategy work is to distinguish possible futures in the here-and-now and to work for the preferred future. In this sense, strategy is more than a plan, road map, or play book. It is a set of recurring activities or practices through which the organization engages with alternative futures – guided by its values. At Moomin, values offer bridges from the past to the future, via the present.

Values derived from the Moomin stories are applied to all four companies within the Moomin Group, regardless of how closely their employees' day-to-day work is connected to the original Moomin books. Managers and employees alike told us that these values lead to a supportive, creative, and joyful environment where everyone is encouraged to do their best work.

Kira Schroeder, a Producer at Moomin Characters, said:

'We know why we exist in this world and how we view the world. And we have an idea of where we want to take the brand. But then the "How do we do it?" is more of a day-to-day negotiation and the tactics of how to implement that strategy is something that, I think, is living every day.'

Our research shows that values underlie how strategy is understood and how strategic choices are made at Moomin. They help explain what we at first found curious and a little surprising: while the everyday functioning of the Moomin ecosystem is well thought out and methodical, and its purpose and purpose-driven values seem crystal-clear, there is little of the elaborate strategy talk – of analyses and plans and of those who are privileged to do strategy – that is characteristic for companies operating in complex and uncertain business environments.

The relatively small size of the core of the Moomin ecosystem offers one explanation for this. In large corporations, elaborate and meticulous strategy work is done to keep the people on the various management levels engaged with the purpose and direction that owners and top management set for the company. This is why frameworks and tools sometimes take over in working with strategy, ensuring that it is done pretty much in the same way throughout the organization and that most if not all have an eye on the same future.

We have not heard fancy talk about balanced scorecards or must-win battles at Moomin, nor have we come across heavy strategy processes or people burdened with endless strategic plans, objectives, and measures. Instead, we witnessed exploration and execution at work.

The lack of excessive strategy talk at Moomin is intriguing because strategy is about dealing with alternative bets on the future. Strategy work is usually laden with vested interests and politics.

Organization and management scholar Martin Kornberger (2013) argues that strategy provides 'the script and the props for a performance of the future in the here-and-now'. It is about disciplining the future, and it transforms time as it mobilizes the future and turns it into a source of power in the present.

In its absolute and all-encompassing glory, then, the chosen strategy – the picture hung on the wall – represents but one possible perspective and bet on the future. It is a specific perspective that prevails over its alternatives. That is why it is always subject to contestation. Who gets to paint in the first place? Whose picture is chosen and on what basis? And what do we do next?

No grand strategy picture can be found at Moomin. There is no detailed strategy document, decided on for once and for all, rigidly followed or grumbled about. While at first glance it seems obvious that Moomin Characters and its business ecosystem can avoid some of the pitfalls in slow, meticulously structured strategic planning, this does not mean that strategy is not done or that strategy work is completely free of conflicting interests and politicking.

"I wouldn't say that Moomin Characters doesn't have a strategy because they do. But it has not been formally written down," a key actor in the Moomin ecosystem told us. "What I think happens is that things occur and that becomes the strategy. It is about reacting fast as opportunities come up. All this makes life interesting." Shared values help guide strategy work at Moomin and give it a sense of purpose and direction. The key question is how the Moomin story and brand – and its purpose and values – is turned into future performance and growth.

Goals are set, of course. Moomin Characters Director of Business Development Thomas Zambra engaged others in discussions on goals and goal setting. At the time of our ethnographic study, the following goals based on the Moomin values were agreed on: (1) fans who carry the brand(s) close to their heart, (2) the most appreciated brand(s), (3) a truly international company, (4) sustainable growth, and (5) happy people.

Goals helped define focus areas for (strategic) action: (1) strengthen the brand narrative, (2) new territories and better clients, (3) ecosystem thinking, (4) all companies profitable, and (5) under one roof. Key performance indicators (KPIs) could then be derived from the goals and focus areas for teams and individuals to steer their work.

"We are moving so quickly so we couldn't make a five-year plan," Kira Schroeder told us. "It's really nice that Moomin is such an agile and organic family company where you can say something at the coffee break, and it's implemented before you get back to your desk because Roleff has called someone as he is walking to his." Kira added, however, that:

'Maybe as the organization grows, there might be a need for more traditional organizational structures and tools like the Monday List.

Sometimes it's been a challenge to know at which stage different projects are. And in the same project, you have different people contacting different levels of the customer's organization. But you don't want endless meetings of updating each other. It's a two-sided coin. It's a strength that we don't have middle managers and procedures, but ...'

The Monday List was something relatively new to Moomin Characters when we began our study (see monday.com). It is an online calendar and planning tool that the core companies in the Moomin ecosystem have adopted to give an overview of the coming year. Week by week, month by month, you can see the name of the project, who is responsible, and which core company is leading it. There are regular meetings and 'side-calendars' to keep the communication flowing, adjusting the focus when needed.

In terms of strategy, this is one place where we witnessed some purposeful planning in Moomin Characters. However, action lists such as this are outcomes of strategy, and the question is, as asked by a key actor in the ecosystem, "Where is the strategy that helps to decide whether to accept or to turn down certain projects?"

There are the Moomin values, and there is a mission statement and a vision as clearly outlined in the internal documents. However, where other companies are trying to articulate a strategy document for 2–5 years, Moomin Characters seems to be leaving it open.

Moomin celebrates their 80th birthday in 2025. "For once," we were told by several people a few years earlier, "the planning has started in good time." Major licensees need two years, in some cases, to pull off a large campaign. Museums and galleries are scheduled years in advance. So, daily work is planned more meticulously than before.

In this structuring of strategy work at Moomin, the next 12 months are planned with the Monday List. And the next 100 years are seen through a vision. But the gap between 2 and 5 years has only a few larger projects in place. This is likely to be on purpose, as most detailed strategy documents go out the window as circumstances change. To be "faster than everyone else," as Moomin Characters CEO Roleff Kråkström said, it may be better to leave the mid-term strategy un-written.

So, overall, it seems that strategy work is kept simple at Moomin. What we see is a form of 'strategy without design', as critical organization scholars Robert Chia and Robin Holt call doing strategy where 'invisible coordinating forces appear to work to bring together fruitful outcomes indirectly and circuitously through a plethora of local coping actions'.

Strategy work at Moomin is emergent, incremental, and oriented towards exploration and execution. At times, but notably seldom, more radical strategic change is pursued. Carefully timed, these purposeful change initiatives offer key learnings that help navigate the business as usual into the future.

★★★

An example of what we consider strategic change at Moomin took place when Roleff Kråkström started as CEO of Moomin Characters in 2008 and when the key decision-makers chose to focus on Tove Jansson's original artwork in developing the Moomin brand and business.

Lots of discussions were held, but we hear of very few disputes having taken place up front. It seems that focusing on Tove's work, (re)positioning Moomin, and clarifying its brand was met with wide support. This strategic change or transformation initiative enabled the Moomin ecosystem to develop into what it is today, and it helped to define and clarify the values as they are now presented.

In an interview with Hyung-Gu Lynn, the editor of *Asia Pacific Memo* in 2016, Roleff Kråkström recited the point of departure for the change initiative. In hindsight, at least, it was about learning to better understand and manage expectations of partners and consumers. 'When we had meetings with licensees, they would invariably ask us whether we had any new film or television series in the works, or perhaps a monster app', Roleff recalled. 'The answer to these questions was that no, we did not have such plans.'

How the entertainment industry functions became clearer and clearer for Moomin decision-makers, and the importance of positioning and differentiating from the competition, to quote the well-known strategy scholar Michael E. Porter, became paramount. With these understandings, Roleff Kråkström and Sophia Jansson were able to offer better justified answers to (potential) licensees, and to engage in negotiations with them regarding collaboration that is mutually beneficial.

Licensing is based on invention of content as well as control of distribution. Roleff and others at Moomin personnel knew that "large entities such as Disney can produce at a specific pulse, where new products flood the market, and the wave lasts for say twelve to twenty-four months, then this is replaced by the next set of products".

Thinking through the competitive positioning of Moomin vis-à-vis the dominant players led to highlighting art as a way of distinguishing from others. Clearly differentiating Moomin from the likes of Disney was deemed crucial, and this is where the notion of art proved useful. Moomin began to carve out their own competitive space, if not the 'blue ocean' beyond competition revered by strategy scholars Renée Mauborgne and W. Chan Kim. Moomin began to purposefully build on distinctive strengths offered by Tove Jansson's work.

Learning to manage stakeholder expectations led to taking stock of competences and capabilities at Moomin, and it crystallized the importance of focus. "We realized that we did not have the resources to compete with such giants in manufacturing entertainment," Roleff said. "We were forced to ask ourselves what makes the Moomins and our company unique? The answer was art. We controlled a body of world-class literature and pictorial art that was licensable."

Deciding on a focus meant reconsidering who to collaborate with. According to Roleff, "We wanted to be true to the original stories and the artwork without being protectors of some ossified heritage that operated on the basis of simply saying no to anything new."

Finding collaborators related to the question of protecting the brand while letting it blossom: "We wanted to work with the most talented people in various artistic fields without being overly aggressive about licensing new styles or new storylines merely to increase the volume of output."

Executing the strategic change helped key decision-makers to learn to deal with balancing acts in managing Moomin as a universally local brand, while staying true to its roots. It helped comprehend strategy as a continuous set of activities, aimed at the future, rather than a one-off event or plan.

This is not rocket science, of course. The purposeful step-by-step approach enabled managers and employees to buy into the newly defined purpose and direction. The fact is that people deal with change initiatives better when they are paced and cut in chunks. Change works better when it is spread out and offered in digestible pieces. How do you eat an elephant? Piece by piece. But you must know what you are eating and why.

This reminds us of management scholar Eric Abrahamson's ideas about what he called change without pain. Abrahamson's point was that a transformation – or revolution – cannot be made every day. Change can hurt, and that is why it needs to be handled with care.

Organizations are advised to live by what Abrahamson termed dynamic stability. He suggested that major change initiatives – transformations or revolutions – are interspersed among carefully placed periods of smaller, organic change.

Revolution is possible, then, but only when there is fertile ground for it and when the revolutionaries know that their efforts will not be toppled by a new revolution the next day. This is what seems to have happened at Moomin in 2008. A transformation was launched and over time it settled into an evolutionary developmental process.

Strategic development is constant. However, it seems that Moomin were embarking upon another transformation at the time of our study when engaging with new technologies and entering virtual worlds became an increasingly important strategic issue. These will be discussed in Chapter 6.

Overall, what we witnessed at Moomin helps to challenge many dogmas and established understandings of what strategy (and strategy work) should be. In traditional understandings, a clear distinction is made between planning and implementation as well as between those who plan and those who are supposed to implement. We saw little of this baggage at Moomin. Instead, the Moomin approach enables a sense of agility that makes change happen fast in practice.

Planning and implementation are difficult to distinguish and set apart in real life, and the distinction seems irrelevant anyway. The relatively small size of the Moomin organization and ecosystem helps to achieve the flexibility or agility needed.

In rethinking the strategic focus and making change happen, according to Roleff Kråkström, "We were fortunate in two respects. First, as a small company, we can make decisions very quickly while assessing proposals for quality and fit. Second, many artists came to us of their own volition to work with us, without us having to commission work. This stemmed in large part from the fact that the original Moomin stories contain all the universal values that any brand could dream of having."

Returning to Tove Jansson's original artwork enabled Moomin to sharpen its purpose and verbalize its values. "Aside from the heraldic imagery and storylines filled with adventure and pensiveness, you can find in Tove Jansson's works love, family, adventure, bravery, tolerance, and loyalty. We didn't have to fabricate these resonances," Roleff summarized the key issues. The 'profound wisdom' was already there, ready to be put into action.

Decision-makers and employees at Moomin learned to appreciate fast execution. However, making the new strategy work also offered a crash course in managing across cultural boundaries. Managing strategically in different cultural circumstances is, and will always be, notoriously difficult. The new strategy developed at Moomin since 2008 was put into action in phases. A conventional procedure was decided on, starting at home before expanding into the most important overseas markets.

'Our Creative Director Sophia Jansson was quite concerned about some of the ways in which the original Moomins had become diluted by some loose depictions. So, we first started in the Nordic countries, where many of our licensees shared our concerns', Roleff Kråkström continued in the interview with *Asia Pacific Memo* back in 2016.

'Predictably, there was a mixed reaction: some of our partners were happy, while others were very worried. But we were able to run several successful projects with designers in these countries before applying the same policies to Japan.'

Japan is the 'second home' for Moomin, and it was a challenge for two reasons. The content of the change was risky because in Japan the Moomins were very much associated with the 1990s animations that were visually different from Tove Jansson's original work.

Also, managing the change successfully meant that it had to be properly localized in cultural circumstances that were assumed to differ from those in Finland and the other Nordic countries. These concerns led Moomin to work closely with local Japanese experts.

In the interview with *Asia Pacific Memo* Roleff recalled:

> In Japan, there was a cluster of steps. Our agent in Japan, Tuttle-Mori, had some merchandizing agreements with third parties. First, we discontinued these. Second, the new companies hired by Tuttle-Mori came in with a blank slate. Third, Mr Takumi Nakayama, who had worked at Disney for many years, joined Tuttle-Mori as a licensing director and was instrumental in hiring staff and designers who were very receptive to our vision. Clear communication and persuasion are, of course, important, but to land a strategy like this unavoidably requires some changes in partners or third-party licensees.

"Tove's images were really not used so much in Japan until around 2010, but today almost all of the images are from the old comic strips," Gustav Melin, long time Bulls executive and a co-founder of Rights & Brands, told us. "We are promoting the use of these images because it's where we see the brand in the future." Today, the approximately 260 Moomin licensees in Japan are an impressive set of companies in a range of industries and businesses.

Strategy works differently in different locations because people have grown used to relating to each other in different ways. They are used to specific forms of interaction (and not others), and they have learned to expect to be managed in specific ways (and not others). Hence the saying 'culture eats strategy for breakfast'.

Local adaptation is also related to what is offered to partners and consumers. Roleff Kråkström told *Asia Pacific Memo* that:

> around 95 % of the content in the official Japanese website is translated from the main version. Fans and bloggers provide much of the content, although we moderate it. Our Japanese partners then translate it, while the rest is locally produced content. We have applied the same template to China and South Korea.

Sensitivity to differences, cultural and other, is crucial for navigating in the increasingly complex global marketplace. Showing respect to people and their different ways of doing things is important. Respect breeds respect. And finding the right (cultural) ways to show respect increases chances of getting people on board in the strategic initiatives as employees, strategic partners, and consumers.

There is a paradox in analysing the success or failure of strategy. While strategy is always oriented to the future, it can be meaningfully analysed only retrospectively, as past endeavours and events, and their outcomes.

★★★

With the benefit of hindsight, the strategic change at Moomin appears to have been a master stroke. It enabled a new competitive positioning in the market, expansion, and profitable growth. It helped root a global and culturally sensitive mindset in the organization and ecosystem.

The strategic change helped Moomin decision-makers to deal with all kinds of ideas, while learning to focus. Most of all, it demonstrated to all the crucial importance of speed and making things happen fast.

These key learnings continue to impact on how strategy is done at Moomin. It reminds us about Henry Mintzberg's (1994) emphasis on strategic thinking rather than meticulous planning.

Roleff Kråkström offered us a rather oracle-like angle to strategy work at Moomin: "We influence and shape things through our choices and decisions. Opportunities fall on our lap, and we package them so that they fit into our story." These are words of wisdom, but they are subject to multiple interpretations.

When strategy is stripped of all its bells and whistles, what remains is a (hopefully clear) purpose and a sense of direction based on which quick but informed decisions can be made regarding where to allocate resources, where to partner, and where to seek profitable growth.

Doing strategy with love, equality, and courage

What makes Moomin unique then? "Because Moomin is a small company and its competitors are all consuming and slow-moving behemoths, Moomin must move faster than the rest to stay ahead," a key actor in the ecosystem summarized its position and purpose.

Strategy work at Moomin evolves and develops, and values of love, equality, and courage act as bridges from the past to the future. They are put into action and strategically managed. Love, equality, and courage are much more powerful than the usual suspects in corporate values such as innovativeness, customer centricity, and performance orientation. They are unique and they help differentiate Moomin from others.

The Moomin Group onboarding booklet tells us that:

Love means that we see and support one another not just as colleagues but as complex human beings with diverse motivations, needs, and lives outside of the office! We try to do Moominmamma proud with the welcome that we give to new starters and new partners. And, importantly, we put great emphasis on respecting and protecting the planet.

To define love as a key value is a bold statement, but against the backdrop of Tove Jansson's life and work as well as the philosophy of the Moomins it is not far-fetched. In fact, it is rather obvious. Love encourages people in the Moomin ecosystem to acknowledge their mutual connections, to respect each other, and to work together in making a better future for all.

Love as a corporate value makes us wonder. It is not something readily associated with strategy – and it is refreshingly original. At Moomin, and against the backdrop of Tove Jansson's creations and life, it makes complete sense.

When we understand love as action rather than as a feeling, following bell hooks, we can foster our love for what we do together. By approaching our joint work with dedication, we can learn to deal with its pleasures and struggles. Understood in this way, love includes willingness, choice, and intention. And like US civil rights movement leader Martin Luther King Jr, who famously said that he had 'decided to love', bell hooks suggested that we choose to love as we choose to act in ways that nurture our own and others' spiritual growth.

bell hooks was an African American author, scholar, educator, and social critic best known for her work on race, feminism, and class. She was born Gloria Jean Watkins and adopted her maternal great-grandmother's name as her pen name because of her snappy and bold tongue. bell hooks styled her name in lowercase letters to convey that what is most important to focus upon is her works, not her personal qualities. She practised what she preached and was a vocal proponent for equality and equity in society. We like to think that bell hooks did generosity through her work.

Choosing love, and deciding to love, seems to characterize the intention behind strategy work at Moomin. This is the first crucial value that connects strategy and generosity. Acknowledging that human beings are complex and different and that they depend on each other offers a sound basis for strategy work at Moomin. Love finds a meaning that helps to further the Moomin purpose and to reach the goals of the organization and ecosystem.

Another Moomin value, equality, 'means that everyone's ideas are welcomed, no matter their seniority or how long they have been working with the company. Our ambition is to foster a culture in which all employees feel able to speak up, share thoughts and opinions, and propose new and alternative ways of working', the Moomin Group onboarding booklet declares. 'As we continue to grow, we hope to recruit widely and diversely, so that we can continue to benefit from new ideas and the varied opinions and experiences of our team members.'

Equality is an equally bold value as love because it implies that organizational members are not only dependent on each other, but they must be treated with equal respect, with equal opportunities to speak up. Creating a psychologically safe (yet brave) community and working environment is based on trust, which in the Nordic countries tends to develop in and through relationships marked by a sense of equal worth. At Moomin, developing mutual trust is made possible by careful people management, which we explore in Chapter 7.

When we observed a Moomin values workshop we realized that equality is about mundane and concrete issues in the organization. When people were summarizing their breakout group discussions, Tiina Liukkonen, Chief Communications Officer at All Things Commerce, said: "One thing we discussed in our small group was workload. Equality in workload. That has a lot to do with planning and daily communication; that everyone is aware of what the others are doing, how they're doing, and how the workload could be dealt out equally."

We also witnessed a wonderful discussion about Ninny, from Tove Jansson's book *The Invisible Child*, and how everyone's work can be made visible: "There are some people who are a bit shier, who do not present their ideas as loudly as others do. So how can we help them out and take this into consideration in our daily work?" This is one reason why some of the sub-planners in the Monday List have been important at Moomin. They help to make everyone's contribution visible. It is not structuring work for its own sake.

One employee said:

'The micro-actions that our group came up with are small things like inviting everyone to join a coffee or lunch, including everyone. Not just that you go with your best friend. If someone asks for help, be there for everyone. When you come to the office, greet everyone, and be encouraging to everyone. Switching languages, to English, Swedish or Finnish, depending on who is in the meeting and what they are comfortable with.'

Extending the discussion to tolerance, Hanna Ahlström from Exhibitions and Artwork Approvals said in the same workshop: "We chose to discuss tolerance and equality. It's about listening even when you disagree with the person. Making sure that everyone has a chance to speak up, so that the loud ones are not the only ones heard."

The discussion on tolerance led to important comments such as "At Moomin Characters, you can come as you are. Being tolerant is also being tolerant with yourself" and "When someone new comes into the company, at least their team should have a dinner and a small party". It was commonly agreed that "we have a party debt for the ones who joined during Covid".

There is no love and equality without courage. The third Moomin value is important because it implies looking into the future together, with confidence, even when feeling confused or scared. Backed by love and equality, courage is the grounding on which the Moomin emphasis on exploration, execution, and fast action stands.

In the values workshop, Fredrik Rahka, CEO of the publishing company Förlaget, said:

'Thinking about tolerance and courage, if you think of the metaphor of having a muscle that you can train, that these are smaller and you can train them over time, so the model should not necessarily be someone else, but it can be how you've been able to handle situations earlier.'

We presume that Fredrik was talking about developing the capability for courage, not thinking too much about big global entertainment companies as competitors but rehearsing to do your own thing and develop your capability to 'handle situations'.

The Moomin onboarding booklet states that:

Courage means a particular mindset. It means seeing challenges and change not as disasters but as opportunities. It means being brave enough to do things differently – not just following the herd or doing things in a certain way because that's how they've always been done. We want our teams and our partners to feel empowered to speak up if they see something they think could be done better, or even to strike out in new directions altogether!

Sharing insights from his group, Thomas Zambra said during the values workshop:

'We focused on courage. We spoke a lot about role models. About acting courageously every day. Making the decisions that have to be made. Not forcing them on others but letting everyone make decisions. Through the example of being courageous, we create an atmosphere where others can be courageous in their work.'

Someone from that group added: "And never selling your colleagues cheap. Always standing up for each other."

Thomas went on: "Making decisions consistently so that people know what to expect and what is expected. We feel courage respects the history of the company and Tove's work. People here are courageous, and people have space to form their own work identity, from one day to the next."

"I think we all agree that we are scared many times, but this work environment pushes us to display courage," Roleff Kråkström added. "That's something that I would like to convey to newcomers. We are all frightened most of the time, but we act bravely."

★★★

Values of love, equality, and courage depend and feed on each other. In arguing for love as doing rather than feeling, bell hooks reminded us that we are all vulnerable. Love helps us to accept our vulnerability, to be brave and to uphold a willingness to stand up for ourselves and for those we care about.

Love engenders hope, hooks said, and our suffering can become a place of peace and possibility. Love and courage are two sides of the same coin, and they prosper in conditions of equality.

Self-acceptance is the foundation of love, but it is always practised within a community. According to bell hooks, love blossoms only if we surrender our attachment to power. The practice of love, then, is revolutionary; it embodies a struggle for justice and freedom.

The braveness and willingness to stand up for ourselves and for those we care about that bell hooks emphasizes come close to how courage is defined at Moomin. It draws on a sense of equal worth and it fosters love in how people behave towards each other.

Taken together, love, equality, and courage offer an intriguing framing for strategy work and for making things happen at Moomin. These values underscore the uniqueness of the Moomin ecosystem and its openness, curiosity, and forward-looking nature. They help to engage with multiple possible futures and to figure out what is likely to happen next.

As the Moomin values suggest, perhaps implicitly, life is not all fun and games. It is also about different (and sometimes incompatible) viewpoints, disputes, and conflicts. Finding ways to discuss and negotiate different views is a key part of strategy work. At Moomin, key decision-makers such as Sophia Jansson and Roleff Kråkström show how you can disagree but still respect each other.

Sophia and Roleff lead by example in that, from time to time, they openly disagree in the monthly meetings, as shown in the heated exchange of words on the new tove.jansson website mentioned earlier. They can continue to disagree and to discuss with one another at the dinner table at home, out of sight of their colleagues, and we were told that this happens often.

While idle values talk in organizations is easy to criticize, and usually for good reason, what we witnessed was something very different. People at Moomin Characters and in the ecosystem seemed to be living the values.

Strategy work seemed to be in many ways grounded in the values that helped steer the organization with an eye on the future.

Working based on love, equality, and courage is a bold statement. It renders the Moomin susceptible to critique and even ridicule. It is the easiest thing in the world to claim that love is lost, equality is elusive, and courage is crushed. Yet, people at Moomin seem to be ready to stand up to the challenge.

Sharpening the approach to sustainability

The Moomin way of doing strategy offers opportunities for engaging with the big questions of our times. As the planet and humankind are facing unprecedented ecological and social challenges, questions of sustainability and responsibility are on the radar of an increasing number of companies and other organizations. Future challenges are in many ways interconnected and call for broad-minded, open, and courageous approaches to management.

Values of love, equality, and courage offer ways for incorporating sustainability and responsibility into Moomin strategy work now and in the future. The Moomin Group onboarding booklet states that: 'Our current focus in terms of the environment is on making sure that sustainability is at the heart of our business and of our cooperation with our licensees, making it as easy as possible for everyone to take practical steps to reduce the environmental impact of our work together.'

There is a lot of talk today in companies about how sustainability, or sustainable development, can be taken as an organizing principle for meeting human and social development goals (such as equality at Moomin) while sustaining the ability of natural systems and the environment to provide the resources on which all societies depend.

At Moomin, this is ingrained in the very ethos of the ecosystem. While Susannah Clapp writing for *The Observer* suggested that Tove Jansson's original Moomin stories from the 1940s and 1950s include visions that today read like warnings of climate change, key Moomin actors today incorporate sustainability and responsibility concerns in the business.

Climate change is just one environmental catastrophe looming over the planet and humankind, alongside biodiversity loss and pollution of seas and oceans. Active engagement in 'Save the Baltic Sea' is an example of how Moomin is doing its bit for the environment.

At the same time, the conviction that sustainability and responsibility are in everything that is done runs the risk of diluting its meaning in the Moomin ecosystem. When sustainability is understood to be everywhere, it can end up being nowhere in particular.

Tightening legislation in the European Union regarding due diligence, auditing, and reporting of corporate sustainability risks encourages companies to increase their engagement and efforts. There are pressures for more transparency in supply chains, and more emphasis on identifying, preventing, and mitigating social responsibility violations.

"How do you advise an amoeba? I heard an insider use the metaphor 'ameoba' to describe the Moomin organization. It is wonderfully organic, with creative people and great enthusiasm and drive," Jessica Jungell-Michelson told us with a smile. "It took us a while to figure out how the Moomin organization works so that we could get our project running."

Jessica and her colleague Sickan Åberg from Sustify Ltd in Finland worked with Moomin Characters and Rights & Brands as external advisors on a strategic sustainability project. Their remit was to help Moomin develop a more structured, systematic, and comprehensive approach to sustainability.

"We first benchmarked forerunner companies in the global licensing business to see how they approach sustainability. At Moomin, we studied documents such as the onboarding booklet, did lots of interviews, and ran a series of workshops," Sickan Åberg recalled. "We have worked with creative people before, but Moomin employees are quite exceptional. They switch roles and multitask. Their level of ambition in sustainability matters is high."

The external advisors put a lot of effort into trying to understand how and why the Moomin ecosystem functions the way it does, to ensure that their recommendations were in line with the Moomin values.

Working with strategic partners such as licensees and their supply chains, for example, was agreed to be a key issue. Monitoring how Moomin merchandise is manufactured and ensuring that environmental standards are retained, and that the safety and the human rights of workers are honoured, in all parts of the supply chains was identified as a timely challenge. One way to deal with this is to include sustainability commitments in licensing contracts.

The Moomin sustainability ambition was defined in the external advisors' final report as 'striving for sustainability leadership in the brand licensing industry'. This was to be achieved through 'brave decisions, collaboration, and transparency'. We could see the Moomin spirit in these formulations. Making sustainability and responsibility into strategic questions of their own, not only taking them seriously but putting more structure around them, is something that Moomin management is faced with now and in the future. This is a highly strategic balancing act because it concerns the future of the world at large.

Companies in general are advised to move beyond ritualistic box-ticking exercises to a more strategic approach to sustainability. In the mediatized global economy, sustainability concerns affect brands and reputations too. Operations management scholar Ruoqi Geng and colleagues' research, among others, shows that media attention affects how companies become aware of the risks in their supply chains and how they address these risks.

Organization and management scholar Paul McGrath and his colleagues, in turn, suggest that more supply chain data and transparency tend to be seen as positive developments for strategic insight and oversight in multinational corporations. However, due to operational challenges, increased costs, and conflicts with other strategic demands such as growth it can be a source of struggle.

Questions of human and social sustainability and responsibility come to the fore alongside care for the environment. This can be understood as a fight against 'modern slavery', which according to public health scholar Elizabeth Such and her colleagues refers to 'the recruitment, movement, harboring or receiving of children, women or men through the use of force, coercion, abuse of vulnerability, deception or other means for the purpose of exploitation'.

Yet, on the one hand, it is too often the case that what is out of sight, is out of mind. Based on their studies, Elizabeth Such and colleagues conclude that significant variation remains in how companies work to avoid infringing on human rights. There is variation in how they address the adverse human rights impact that their operations may have in less privileged parts of the world.

On the other hand, there is mounting pressure put by policy makers, media, and other stakeholders on companies to regularly monitor and assess their human rights impact. Investors and other owners can be at the forefront of such developments for making businesses more sustainable.

Environmental, social, and governance (ESG) standards recommend taking environmental issues, social issues, and corporate governance issues into account when investing in companies. ESG can be used by investors as a systematic set of frameworks and procedures to holistically assess a company's sustainability efforts and societal impact. For this, they need detailed and up-to-date information, which puts the screws on companies to offer more of such information.

A study by the executive search and leadership consultancy Heidrick & Struggles indicated that company boards in Europe are putting increasing focus on sustainability in their strategic decision-making. There is also evidence to suggest that the owners' voice is translated into the strategic agenda of CEOs. A study by Climate Leadership Coalition, for example, showed that Nordic business leaders are concerned about climate change and its consequences and that they are prepared to collaborate with policy makers on sustainability issues.

Whichever way they are viewed, sustainability and responsibility are crucial and far-reaching strategic challenges for Moomin to tackle. The grounding for this is in place, we think.

★★★

As external advisors, Jessica Jungell-Michelsson and Sickan Åberg helped Moomin employees look at sustainability from different angles. Eventually, they helped Moomin craft a sustainability roadmap. "This reflects their high level of ambition," Jessica told us. "We discussed where to go and how to get there, and the roadmap identifies where to focus now and in the future. It is grounded in the Moomin values."

The focus areas in the sustainability roadmap are (1) build to last (working towards longer lasting products through recyclability, circularity, and sustainable design and materials in products and packaging), (2) love for nature (working towards minimized negative impact on nature through reduced environmental footprints and increased use of sustainable and recycled materials), and (3) roadmap to happiness (maximizing the positive social and cultural impacts of the Moomin values and stories, internally and externally). Targets and goals were set for each focus area, and actions to reach them were specified.

Based on the external experts' recommendations, key actors in the Moomin ecosystem are sharpening their strategic approach to sustainability. "We have been pretty lousy in some sustainability questions. We understand our shortcomings and challenges, however, and aim to do better," Roleff Kråkström confirmed.

'We focus on what we are good at, and we do our best to get experts on board who can help us develop in areas where we do less well. We get around and meet a lot of people all the time. We constantly scan for experts to help us. Let's face it – Moomin is an environmental hazard. What I mean is that stuff is manufactured with our licenses that humankind and the globe do not need. … We always go for a bold approach in everything we do. We do not try to avoid mistakes but learn from them. The main goal now with sustainability is that we become more systematic. We identify the most acute issues and keep them on our radar.'

One key issue relates to working with licensees as strategic partners. Local manufacturing and localized supply chains are encouraged. Many markets where Moomin have a strong position are democracies with an understanding of sustainability related concerns. Consumers in educated middle classes in these markets are worried about the state of the world and want to do their bit. This offers a grounding for Moomin to work on sustainability with licensees.

At the same time, partners such as Oxfam, WWF, and Amnesty International monitor Moomin operations all the time. "They don't work with those who are ignorant," Roleff said. The Moomin ecosystem has engaged in long-term strategic collaboration with global and local not-for-profit organizations, and Moomin is in the limelight to make sure it takes sustainability seriously.

Moomin now collaborates with Lune Climate Ltd that offers software for emission calculations and carbon offsetting projects. Tapping into Lune's expertise, Moomin headquarters in Helsinki is committed to reducing its carbon footprint to the value of 100,000 euros per year. This is related to the external advisors' recommendation for Moomin to continuously assess and improve the impacts of their internal processes.

New technologies overall help tackle sustainability challenges and there are many exciting companies to collaborate with. For example, Infine is a Finnish technology start-up that is focused on transforming their clients' product and service data into 'easy-to-comprehend' sustainability insights.

On their website, Infine offers 'science-based product sustainability management for companies selling or producing food, textiles, household items and consumables'. They promise tools that yield sustainability insights for their clients through 'deep tech, automation, AI, and industrial-size scalability'. Infine's science-based tools can be used to detect and avoid risks, spot opportunities, and lead growth.

"A key point of development for us is to take this kind of thinking to our licensees and to offer them incentives to be more sustainable. For example, we can reward with lower royalty payments those licensees who score well in sustainability," Roleff Kråkström told us. "We don't do it for brownie points in media and marketing. We do it because we care."

In defining the value of love, the Moomin onboarding booklet notes that 'we put great emphasis on respecting and protecting the planet'. In practice, environmental and social sustainability concerns intertwine. When the planet is well, people are well, and vice versa. Love, combined with equality and courage, helps define an ethical compass that serves to direct business operations strategically at Moomin.

Strategizing generously

Strategy work at Moomin is original, to say the least, but it resonates with the more non-mainstream research in the area. How working with strategy is set up at Moomin, what priorities guide it, and how it is grounded in values and a sense of purpose speaks to dynamic understandings of strategy.

Well-known organization and management scholar James G. March proposed exploration and exploitation as key concepts to make sense of balancing acts in how organizations function and are strategically managed. Exploration is about searching for new ideas, or innovativeness, while exploitation is about old certainties and making efficient use of what we (think we) already know. One is about investing in the future, the other about capitalizing on past investments.

The trick is that too much exploration makes you lose track of what you have that is worth preserving. Too much exploitation, in turn, petrifies the organization and keeps it from spotting strategic opportunities. You must seek to get that balance right every day.

The notion of balancing acts keeps coming up when we analyse the Moomin ecosystem. Exploration seems to be a fundamentally important feature of how strategy is done at Moomin. New opportunities are constantly scanned and taken up.

The other side of the coin is execution. The sustainability advisors Jessica Jungell-Michelsson and Sickan Åberg, for example, were mesmerized by the speed with which they were hurled into the organization. "Determination and fast pace were characteristic of the whole project," Sickan recalled. The strategic need for looking into sustainability was identified and no time was lost in getting to work.

Quick decisions and execution characterize the Moomin ecosystem. This is not without its risks, of course. Sometimes decisions can be made too quickly, without due consideration of their overall consequences.

Moomin seems to operate like the 'emerging-market multinationals' that boundary-crossing management scholars Mauro F. Guillén and Esteban García-Canal studied. They argue that the Western obsession with creating complicated and fancy strategic plans becomes obsolete in the fast pace of doing business in Asia, the Middle East, and Latin America.

Emerging-market multinationals originating outside the West seize opportunities even if significant risks are involved, 'adapting their goals in real time', as Guillén and García-Canal put it. Instead of fantastic plans, the strategic challenge is to secure a firm grip on the day-to-day realities of operations.

What makes exploration and fast execution in the Moomin ecosystem special is the grounding in values that encourage generosity in strategy work. "We ask all our employees and partners to remember our values of love, equality and courage, and be committed to enacting them through our work, our conversations and the choices we make," the Moomin Group onboarding booklet concluded. "It falls to all of us at the Moomin Group to make sure we are working as sustainably as possible, so if you notice something that could be done better, please speak up!"

★★★

Generosity 'for generations to come' takes the form of managing with purpose and vision at Moomin. Living the values of love, equality, and courage means that they are not only taken seriously but used to guide business decisions.

Generosity is what generosity does: talk is not enough to convince the key stakeholders. In Moomin strategy work, generosity helps steer the future. This increasingly incorporates questions of sustainability and responsibility, although putting more structure around approaching them is a constant challenge. Generosity here is about tangible and intangible resources and capabilities, relations, and ways of doing things.

Moomin strategy work is seemingly without design. Yet, there is a specific way of talking about strategy that guides their operations and steers the ecosystem into the future.

In their study of (lack of) participation in corporate strategy work, organization and management scholars Saku Mantere and Eero Vaara elucidate how in some companies strategy is talked about as if it were a secret art reserved for the chosen few, that is, those who know better than others and who have earned the right to be involved in strategy work.

When the time comes for the others to enjoy the fruits of the strategists' labour – in other words, when strategy is 'communicated' to them – it is no wonder that little happens. Strategy remains detached from the everyday realities of people in the organization. It remains a mystery at best, and a punishment at worst, Mantere and Vaara argue.

This does not seem to be the case in the Moomin ecosystem. Many people are involved in doing strategy and impacting upon the future. To be involved is more than to participate. Involvement means caring about and, perhaps, loving what you do.

The challenge is to involve and engage people – all the creative role-switchers and multi-taskers – in building the business and embracing the values of love, equality, and courage. This entails openness and transparency that is sometimes hard to accomplish because of (prospective) partners' needs for confidentiality and secrecy.

As organization and management scholars, we know that managing through strong values can play out as a form of control. Peter Fleming and Andrew Sturdy, among others, critically scrutinize new forms of exploiting workers in vulnerable positions. They elucidate how workers today are forced to embrace their work wholeheartedly and to have 'fun' while carrying out their tasks under strict surveillance. Michelle Mielly, Gazi Islam, and Dora Gosen elaborate on this 'neo-normative control' and show how it calls for a positive affective disposition toward work. They argue, however, that it is often accompanied by diffuse and persistent anxiety, fear, and other forms of suffering.

No matter how we twisted and turned it, we could not see that Moomin values were used for exploiting people in the ecosystem. They did not appear as a coercive form of control, although they seemed to have an impact on how people engaged with the Moomin brand and strategy work. There were some side effects, complicating relations and interaction between people at Moomin, and we return to these in Chapter 7.

Overall, we found that strategy work at Moomin fostered a sense of purpose and belonging. So, we are back to Henry Mintzberg (1994) and his ideas on strategic thinking. To be meaningful, 'thinking' cannot be reserved for the chosen few. It needs to be voiced and subjected to dialogue, as is done at Moomin Characters and the ecosystem.

Strategizing generously means involving more people and extending the pool of strategists at Moomin. It does not mean that no-one is in charge, however. Someone is always ultimately responsible for the decisions made – this is defined by law. This someone must take responsibility for defining the purpose, choosing the direction, and setting goals. But this someone also needs to have the courage to share the burden with others.

Strategy work is not without tensions and conflicts, within the ecosystem and with strategic partners. As Roleff Kråkström told us: "We can be quite ruthless, and this enables us to be generous. We are good at fighting and in making up. We have this prankster mentality, something that Tove Jansson also had. We allow ourselves to do a good deal if it helps us to do good."

Figure 5.1: Mymble turning things upside down

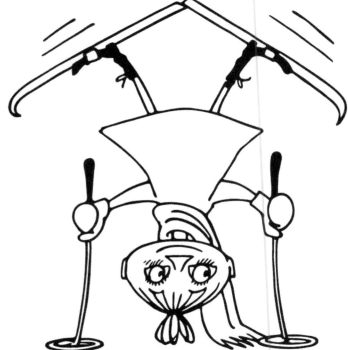

Source: © Moomin Characters™

Different viewpoints and disputes add spice to the boldness of strategy work at Moomin. Questions of purpose and direction are sometimes heatedly argued. At the same time, different meanings of generosity are constantly debated. What generosity means is never solved once and for all. Like strategy, generosity is a continuous journey. Its meanings are negotiated and redefined over time.

This comes to the fore when Moomin Characters expands its digital footprint and offering and extends generosity to the virtual sphere. Next, we turn to how technologies and people work together in the digitalized and mediatized global economy. We explore initiatives by Moomin based on new technologies and the opportunities they offer.

6

Technologies: Into Virtual Worlds

'New Moomin game by creators of Angry Birds in development. Iconic Finnish brands will join forces to create joyful content for years to come as Rovio becomes an exclusive partner for Moomin based mobile games', the Moomin website announced in June 2021. 'Rovio's first Moomin game, based on the original story and world created by Tove Jansson and inspired by the *Moominvalley* animation visuals, is already being developed.'

Moomin Characters, Rovio Entertainment, and Gutsy Animations launched their new long-term partnership with high hopes. They made public their joint intention to develop and market a new game for smart phones and expand into games across platforms. The partnership was envisioned to open new opportunities for the Moomin trademark, in line with the objective of 'taking local Nordic creations to the international marketplace'.

A couple of years earlier, Moomin had engaged in another ambitious venture that made use of opportunities offered by new technologies. The *Moominvalley* animation television series in 3D was first released in 2019. This high-profile initiative included collaboration with global corporations. Through Gutsy Animations, Moomin partnered with major actors in the entertainment and media business.

The new *Moominvalley* animations marked a new phase in the development of the ecosystem, and initiatives such as a collaboration with Rovio on mobile games follow this trajectory. The eyes of Moomin management are increasingly on technology and digitalization. With the new initiatives, Moomin is embracing new opportunities to 'scale its digital footprint' and to discover new markets and attract new clients around the world.

In managerial talk, digitalization typically refers to leveraging digital technologies to change and transform ways of doing business, and to create new revenue streams and value-creating opportunities. Digital disruption is a concept used to denote the radical changes in expectations and behaviour that digitalization engenders. This pertains to new technologies and, most notably today, to artificial intelligence (AI).

In making sense of AI and its impact, organization and innovation scholar Georg Von Krogh steers our focus to decision-making and problem-solving. He concludes that AI augments rather than substitutes human behaviour in organizations. Von Krogh foresees a fertile ground ahead for discovering unexpected combinations of human ingenuity with intelligent machines.

In this spirit, and following research by technology and innovation scholars Samer Faraj and Stella Pachidi, we are interested in the co-constitutive relation between new technologies and organizing at Moomin. This means that we view technologies and people in organizations as interrelated, and not as separate entities. Technologies are, according to Faraj and Pachidi, 'endogenous to and constitutively entwined with organizational actions and structures'.

So, technologies impact upon people and ways of organizing and managing, which in turn impact upon the further development and use of technologies, and so forth. We refer to these processes as digitalizing. Rather than technologies themselves, our focus is on technologies and people and how they (fail to) work together at Moomin.

In this chapter, we highlight how Moomins are taken to the virtual sphere and explore Moomin and new technologies more generally. Among other things, technological developments today are about Big Data, AI, and robots, and these are not all equally relevant for Moomin. Choices and decisions must be constantly made.

As Moomin Characters is scaling its digital footprint, generosity is extended to new environments, and it is entangled with functionalities of technologies. New technologies not only offer opportunities for values-based business in the Moomin ecosystem but provide acute challenges for retaining Tove Jansson's spirit and values. Digitalizing generously seems to be a trial-and-error process where the coherence of the Moomin story is put to the test.

Expanding into the unknown

"We know what we think is right, but when they show us what they have understood, we negotiate and compromise," Sophia Jansson commented on how Moomin Characters worked back and forth with Gutsy over the look, feel, and content of the *Moominvalley* animation series. "We stand firm on the critical parts, but we have to accept that there are different ways to see this story."

The Moomins sense of curiosity and adventure comes in handy in moving into digital and virtual worlds. The Moomin value of courage is needed because it is in many ways about expanding into the unknown. Unchartered terrains await the curious traveller, like in Tove Jansson's Moomin stories.

Many surprises are to be expected in engaging with digitalization, or the use of digital technologies in providing new revenue and value-producing opportunities. The question of strategically moving to digital businesses is a delicate one.

Collaboration with Rovio seems like a logical move in this journey, and the strategic partnership makes sense. While Rovio Entertainment Corporation is a global company, it has strong Finnish roots. Rovio is best known for the global Angry Birds brand, which started as a popular mobile game in 2009.

Rovio is a 'mobile-first games company' that creates, develops, and publishes mobile games that have been downloaded billions of times. Rovio has evolved from games to entertainment and consumer products in brand licensing. The partnership with Moomin Characters was scheduled to run until 2027.

In 'iconic Finnish brands' joining hands, Moomin is an attractive partner for Rovio due to its high brand awareness in Japan, which is one of the largest gaming markets in the world. Through the partnership, Rovio acquired the rights to develop and publish games based on Moomin intellectual property for any platform, with exclusive rights for all mobile platforms.

Through an equity investment and a convertible loan, Rovio also became a minority shareholder in Gutsy Animations, the creator of the *Moominvalley* 3D animation series. This was also expected to spur collaboration and joint initiatives beyond Moomin.

In 2020, following the successful collaboration in making the *Moominvalley* series, the Jansson family-run Moomin Characters and Bulls Holding AB, parent company of Bulls Press and Rights & Brands, took minority stakes in Gutsy Animations alongside other investors. Roleff Kråkström said: "Gutsy Animations is a great fit to our cultural ecosystem, which has been developed around Moomin Characters over the years."

The spirit of discovery was carried over to collaboration with Rovio. 'Gutsy Animations did an astonishing job at bringing to life the rich stories and alluring atmosphere of the Moominvalley. We are honoured and excited to enter this partnership with Moomin Characters and Gutsy Animations', Alex Pelletier-Normand, CEO of Rovio, said in the press release in June 2021. 'Working with Gutsy and Moomin will give us the opportunity to present this iconic brand to new audiences across the globe at the same time as we surely will delight our existing fans.'

Marika Makaroff, Founder and Chief Creative Officer of Gutsy Animations, added in the press release: 'I'm thrilled to have Rovio joining us and bolstering our efforts to create meaningful international content that leans into Nordic values.' Makaroff went on to argue that 'this investment shows growth does not always need to come from far afield and is an incredible display of confidence in Gutsy Animations' ability to create high quality, distinctive content for the global market'.

'By forging a collaboration between three Finland-based companies, this partnership shows a high level of trust in Finnish know-how, highlighting the power of storytelling through shared values', Marika Makaroff concluded. 'Through this investment, we'll have a valuable opportunity to continue writing Finnish success stories across the worlds of both entertainment and culture, which follow in the footsteps of our celebrated, Emmy® Award-nominated adaptation of the original Moomin stories, *Moominvalley*.'

Moomin aimed to benefit from the collaboration by expanding their presence and offering in digital environments. Roleff Kråkström emphasized the wealth of expertise and success Rovio has in this area. There also seemed to be strategic rationale for the partnership that goes beyond Moomin: "We're confident this partnership will open up new opportunities not only to the Moomin trademark, but also to the additional Nordic story. This partnership marks an important milestone in our strategy to take local Nordic creations to the international marketplace."

Scaling a business means adding revenue at a faster rate than taking on new costs. Digitalization offers ample opportunities for this: once the digital product is up and running, it can in principle be spread endlessly with little extra cost.

Scaling is a popular concept in technology-related businesses where commitment to growth is imminent and the right technological innovations enhance growth through scalability. Scaling the Moomin 'digital footprint' is an integral part of the business rationale behind the new technologically driven initiatives such as developing games with Rovio, which was acquired by the Japanese gaming giant Sega in the autumn of 2023.

At the time of our ethnographic study, key decision-makers such as Roleff Kråkström and Thomas Zambra seemed to embrace the opportunities offered by new technologies, and the spirit was widely shared within the ecosystem. People at Moomin were thinking hard about what it means to recreate a two-dimensional world as three-dimensional. They also seemed to be aware of the risks involved in these endeavours.

The collaboration with Rovio began to bear fruit. In December 2021, Rovio launched a new puzzle game titled *Moomin: Puzzle & Design* for early access for Android in Finland. The game has a unique storyline based on Moominmamma's love of gardening. The idea is that Moomins have slept out the winter, the Moominvalley is ready to bloom again, and players solve various puzzles and decorate the valley with flowers, bushes, and other items.

Rovio's interim report for the first quarter of 2023 established that 'great progress' was made with *Moomin: Puzzle & Design*, which 'showed promising results in the mid-term retention test in the Japanese market in Q1, remaining on track for global launch'. Soft launch tests in specific markets continued and new content was added to the game. The global launch was planned for spring 2024.

The game includes tap-to-match puzzles on different levels with unique challenges, some harder than others. On clearing four or more matches, the players get a power booster. The players can then use boosters, combos, and puzzle-solving skills to clear the toughest puzzle. These kinds of elements are typical for games and gamified environments where people get used to gathering points, to receiving badges for their accomplishments, and to monitoring their points and scores in competition with others.

Moomin's collaboration with Rovio offers a glimpse into the intricacies of gamification. Gaming scholar Juho Hamari argues that gamification activates people to gather points (P), compete for acknowledgement or badges (B), and keep an eye on their ranking on leaderboards (L). This forms the holy triad of the touted 'PBL' approach in gamification.

Confronting this competitive ethos, Moomin generosity is put to the test when it is gamified in online spaces. Ultimately, gamification is about applying elements of game playing to other areas of activity. It is a powerful play-derived managerial practice for (re)designing work and organizing. Time will tell how gamification affects management and generosity at Moomin.

★★★

Collaboration with Rovio is but one recent example of the Moomin ecosystem's growing engagement with digitalization. The *Moominvalley* animation television series in 3D first released in 2019 was a significant learning experience in terms of making use of cutting-edge technologies. New seasons of the series followed.

From the point of view of Moomin management, this meant re-interpreting the traditional two-dimensional world of the Moomins. Flat comic strips and book illustrations required some physical changes as characters begin to move their arms and legs, mouths, and tails in a flowing manner that is not present in a 2D world. This is about placing Tove Jansson's work in a new medium and requires flexibility.

For Moomin Characters, collaboration with Gutsy Animations has been a major part of the learning process. In return, the Gutsy website proudly presented *Moominvalley* as their signature achievement: 'Directed to a family primetime audience, the drama fantasy series is full of life and laughter for lifelong Moomin fans, and complete newcomers alike.'

We were told that in 2017 Gutsy Animations organized a crowdfunding campaign on Indiegogo's platform to raise funds for the visual development of the *Moominvalley* series. The campaign brought together some 3,700 Moomin fans. With help from the backers, a distinct visual design in 3D computer generated imagery was created.

Producing the animation series, too, was a huge collaborative effort. There were hundreds of professionals in animation, music, voice acting, visual storytelling, sales, marketing, production, and other experts working together to make the series a reality.

Moomin collaboration with Rovio and Gutsy shows how new technologies and digitalization are intricately intertwined with mediatization, and how managing their connections becomes increasingly complex and difficult.

Mediatization refers to processes by which the mass media and, increasingly, social media are influencing other sectors of society and business. Media logics of attention seeking and sharp representations conquer ground everywhere.

Media logics are at play in games and in animations. In producing and distributing mobile games, the Moomin brand is taken to new environments and to new associations. It is increasingly difficult to protect the brand in online spaces where consumers interact with it in real time.

Taken to the extreme, how the Moomins look and how they act are at the mercy of how players choose to engage with them. Consumers of mobile games expect to be able to interact with the game as well as with other players. At the same time, the Moomin brand is now tied to and associated with Rovio and its game brands.

In producing and distributing an animation series, in turn, the Moomin brand is faced with distinct challenges. Apart from negotiating and making compromises on how accurately the series follows Tove Jansson's stories and visuals, Moomin liaises with global players in the music business and performing arts and gets entangled in webs of connections that are difficult to control and predict.

Basing the Moomin brand on art rather than entertainment is, perhaps inescapably, compromised in these webs of connections and associations. The Moomins look and feel a little different from the originals, and different Moomin clients and fans are likely to have different views on the extent to which computer graphics can be considered as art.

★★★

Direct and indirect collaborations with major global corporations are a part of Moomin's new initiatives. For example, Sony Music label Columbia Records provided the soundtrack for the *Moominvalley* series.

According to *Music Business Worldwide*, Ferdy Unger-Hamilton, president of Columbia Records UK, said in 2018 that they were proud to collaborate as 'the Moomins are culturally important around the world'. He also applauded the 'fantastic line-up of artists across Sony Music Entertainment contributing featured songs to the soundtrack'.

The official soundtrack for the first season of *Moominvalley* included original recordings from an impressive set of artists such as Tom Odell, First Aid Kit, Alma, Delilah Montagu, Declan McKenna, MØ, and SOAK. Moomin attracted many well-known performers, and the outcome was a 'high-profile music entertainment' package.

The cast of actors giving their voices to the Moomin family and friends in the *Moominvalley* series was equally impressive. Taron Egerton was Moomintroll, Rosamund Pike Moominmamma, and Matt Berry Moominpappa. Academy Award and Grammy Award winner Kate Winslet performed as Fillyjonk. The cast also included an exquisite selection of top British comedians, including Jennifer Saunders as Mymble, Will Self as Muskrat, and Matt Lucas as Teety-woo. Richard Ayoade enjoyed spooking viewers as the somewhat un-scary The Ghost.

The series was directed by Steve Box, who among other things has an Academy Award under his belt. In the UK, the *Moominvalley* series aired on Sky One and Sky's on-demand service NOW TV.

In Japan, the series aired on the national broadcaster NHK, and voices included well-known actors such as Ikue Ôtani, Kikuko Inoue, Issey Takahashi, and Yasunori Matsumoto. Both the production and distribution of the series were carried out with high ambition and quality in the key Moomin markets.

The first *Moominvalley* series received a lot of media and social media attention, and it was noted by professional communities. *Moominvalley* won the TBI Content Innovation Awards for Best Animated Kids Program in 2019 and the British Animation Award for Best Children's Series in 2020. And, of course, it was nominated for International Emmy® Kids Awards in 2020.

A lot of the media attention was positive, but not all were equally impressed. Joel Golby, writing for *The Guardian*, said that he 'always got slightly disconcerted by the Moomins'. Golby's gentle criticism of *Moominvalley* was based on the assertion that 'they always made me nervous as a boy and, if we're being honest, still do now'. Golby lamented that 'the original Moomins series more or less split the children who watched it into two adult camps: those who are still filled with a deep abyss of dread (me), or those who still buy Moomin-themed cups and Moomin-themed plates and Moomin plushies, even though they're 40'.

With the *Moominvalley* animation series and collaboration with Rovio, Moomin is joining the big leagues in the digitalized and mediatized global economy. Boundaries between art and entertainment become increasingly blurry from the perspective of the Moomin strategy, business, and brand. Engaging with new technologies, Moomin gets entangled not only in the entertainment business but media too. Staying true to its roots, nurturing its art-based brand, and, crucially, retaining the spirit of generosity in everything that is done, is a key challenge for Moomin in engaging with new technologies.

★★★

Moomin is in many ways involved in virtual worlds. In 2018, Moomin Characters and the Finnish virtual reality studio Zoan announced their collaboration to create Moomin characters in virtual reality. The goal was that Moominvalley can be visited by putting on a virtual reality headset, whether one happens to be in a café in Helsinki or a department store in Tokyo. Moomin clients and fans could enjoy a new experience at their leisure.

"The global demand for virtual characters is growing, and we want to be one of the pioneers by introducing the Moomins into virtual reality. Zoan convinced us as a pioneer in the field, and it felt natural to choose a Finnish partner," said Roleff Kråkström. The visual solutions in Moomin virtual reality were based on the characters created by Gutsy Animations for the *Moominvalley* animated series, first released in 2019.

Virtual reality refers to 3D-modelled artificial reality. It is based on models of the Moomin characters and Moominvalley as well as a game engine. Due to its interactivity, virtual reality differs from videos. Instead of just watching, users can take part in adventures in the virtual worlds.

The same Moomin elements are used in augmented reality where a mobile phone can be pointed at an image that 'comes to life' on the phone screen. In 2019, Moomin Characters began to collaborate with health services company Mehiläinen in Finland in renewing their Mehiläinen for Children brand.

This collaboration aimed at creating a new kind of visibility for children's medical services. Moomin and Mehiläinen joined forces with Zoan and Arilyn, creator of augmented reality experiences, to cheer up kids waiting for their turn at the hospital.

Augmented reality ignited posters with Moomin characters were put on walls of hospital waiting rooms all over Finland. Moomins came to life when children and parents visiting the hospital scanned the posters with the Arilyn app. When scanned, the posters ignited into augmented reality portholes and opened different views and story settings in the Moominvalley.

From the posters, users could explore, for example, what Moominmamma's purse hides and what pearls of wisdom are lurking in Moominpappa's hat. The Moomin purpose of doing good and being generous while doing business came to life in new ways.

New Moomin video game adaptations were also under way. *Snufkin – Melody of Moominvalley* was an indie game developed by the award-winning Norwegian games studio Hyper Games. In this game, Snufkin and his friends needed to restore nature and defend Moominvalley against the strict Park Keeper in the musical puzzle adventure.

"Our decision is that the characters in Moomin video games can only do things that would be done in Moominvalley," Thomas Zambra, Moomin Characters Director of Business Development, recited the brand management aspects of the new digitalization initiatives. "We will not see just any genre of video games." Tove Jansson's principle of not associating the Moomins with religion, politics, violence, or sex is consequently still being adhered to.

The temptation to exploit the brand is accentuated in virtual worlds and when looking to scale the Moomin digital footprint. Thomas pondered a couple years ago: "People are approaching us regarding the metaverse. They talk about nonfungible tokens or NFTs, and how much money we could make with them. Unbelievable numbers … and I'm not sure those numbers are correct. Does this fit with our brand, and if so, how exactly?"

Nonfungible tokens represent assets digitally. This includes online-only assets like digital artwork and in-game items like avatars, digital and non-digital collectibles, and domain names. More and more artists were auctioning tokens to their unique virtual works a few years back, and many seemed to be interested in purchasing them. Various kinds of NFT deals worth billions of euros were made.

Thomas concluded:

> 'We have been monitoring what is going on and talking to experts in the field. The proposal we heard several times is a digital version of Moominvalley that you could visit. Not like a tour, but freely going around and living there somehow. I think that is outside our brand, at least how the metaverse is presented to us. We will see how all this develops and consider our position again if necessary.'

This seems like a sound approach. The NFT market looks very different today than it did some time ago. The virtual world is a complex one, to put it mildly, and difficult to predict. New risks as well as opportunities arise for businesses.

There are also other challenges with new technologies. A global do-it-yourself culture has emerged where consumers and fans want to create and share their own content online. The question is how does brand management play out when fans start to create their own virtual Moomin worlds? The jury is still out.

Opportunities (and challenges) seem endless with new technologies. It is advisable to keep a cool head in expanding into digital and virtual worlds. It is easy to get carried away with technologies and forget about people. This is yet another balancing act that Moomin management is faced with, today and tomorrow.

People, technologies, and magic

According to renowned science fiction writer Arthur C. Clarke, any sufficiently advanced technology is indistinguishable from magic. Technologies have always had a flirting relationship with what to us mortal humans appear to be magical. The promise of new technologies is typically sold to us as radically disruptive.

Organization and management scholar Dirk Lindebaum and his colleagues argue that new technologies of AI can generate self-inflicted states of learned helplessness in us humans. As laymen, we are awed by technologies, and we are strangely disarmed and docile when confronted with their assumed disruptive potential.

As the earlier examples show, however, Moomin *is* changing with new technologies and their 'magic'. It is how technologies and people work together that is the crucial prerequisite for success. By 'people' we do not only mean those who develop technologies, but those who use them too.

Taking a step beyond specific initiatives that engage with new technologies, we can detect some underlying currents in developments that Moomin are tackling. This leads us to view Big Data, AI, and robots strategically and to consider how Moomin aim to harness them in business operations now and in the future.

Big Data forcefully entered management and business vocabulary and practice some 10–15 years ago. It was a term used for data sets so large and complex that traditional tools and data processing applications could not handle them. Digital economy and AI experts Andrew McAfee and Erik Brynjolfsson famously argued for incorporating the finding, sorting out, and translating huge chunks of all kinds of data in organizations and management.

McAfee and Brynjolfsson shook up established ways of thinking and acting in companies and other organizations. They argued that Big Data is worthless if we do not know what to do with all the information we get. McAfee and Brynjolfsson encouraged us to stop pretending to be more data-driven than we are. We were advised to develop evidence-based practices that offer the right people opportunities to ask the right questions in a timely manner.

To build an organization – and at Moomin, a business ecosystem – that is receptive to capitalizing on the wealth of information on offer, McAfee and Brynjolfsson suggested that we must first get rid of 'HiPPO', not the Moomins of course, but the 'highest-paid person's opinion'. Relying on the top strategists' hunches is what many organizations do as a matter of course, and this can be a drag on success.

According to McAfee and Brynjolfsson, Big Data calls for a mindset change on the part of top strategists who must learn to allow themselves to be overruled by the data, to swallow their pride, and to make decisions based on evidence instead of intuition.

At Moomin, the new ventures and initiatives discussed previously were all based on research and data on what consumers do and expect and on what is possible to do with technologies. Data analytics play into most if not all operations in the Moomin ecosystem. As the Director of Business Development at Moomin Characters, Thomas Zambra and his team have been preoccupied with developing the right metrics as well as new product and service offerings for licensees and consumers.

According to Andrew McAfee and Erik Brynjolfsson, the questions that must be asked include: Where's the evidence? What does the data say? Where does the data come from? How was the analysis conducted? By whom? And based on what assumptions?

There is an increasing number of people in different roles in the Moomin ecosystem who are dealing with these questions on a daily basis. In a blog published a few years ago on seobuddy.com, Erica Terranova from the marketing team at All Things Commerce shared her insights on digital efforts at Moomin, including search engine optimization or 'SEO'. In her account, measures and measuring were promptly entangled with business development.

When Erica Terranova's blog was published in May 2021, Moomin was said to have '2,843 referring domains, including a lot of important publications like The Guardian and The New York Times'. This, Erica wrote, was due to a 'focus on brand integrity and brand values' that 'has helped build a strong reputation'.

Referring domains are websites from which the target website or web page has one or more backlinks. This is yet another example of the importance of connections and associations in the digitalized and mediatized global economy.

Keeping score of connections helps to position Moomin in the market. Erica Terranova said that 'we have little control on which sites link back to us, so we tend to focus on organic quality link-building to counteract unavoidable toxic domains. What this means in practice is that we focus on writing great content.'

Erica added that apart from creating 'great content' Moomin constantly seeks to improve its measurement capabilities: 'we are now able to measure the performance of our shop and website combined, or separately so that we can track the performance of every blog post also in terms of sales.'

Once you think you have found a formula that works, it is tempting to keep repeating the same thing. 'We all know how algorithms updates can suddenly change everything, but, more generally, the only way to find new avenues for growth is to keep testing new things', Erica Terranova concluded. Change is constant, and testing is endless in the digitalized world.

All this puts a spin on the power of generosity at Moomin. Measurement and metrics cannot be avoided, but they must act as servant, not master. They help steer generosity but must not be let to determine it. However, in the brand-centred and values-based Moomin business, metrics and measurement taking over is a distinct risk. People are still needed to make judgements on what is feasible and what is not, and why, and to decide on what will be done and what not. Data analytics are complemented by human insight. Hence, Erica Terranova's focus on creating 'great content'.

With wrong choices, the exciting and coherent constellation of branding, partnerships, and strategy work in the Moomin ecosystem can tremble and fall like a house of cards. Aiming to take advantage of all new opportunities that technologies can promise can end up in suboptimization and chaos.

Human discretion is needed in managing the business strategically and responsibly – and in retaining the coherence in the Moomin brand. This is yet another example of the co-constitutive relation between new technologies, people, and organizing.

Digitalization is not only about Big Data and its interpretation, of course. New technologies are connected to developments in AI more generally. Again, there is a lot of hype around AI. Cutting-edge technologies tend to be legitimized as objects of desire that contain a radical promise of disruption that transforms organizations and organizing.

AI is typically construed as disruptive. Organization and management scholars Mikko Vesa and Janne Tienari maintain that the idea of disruption is powerful because it shapes public perception of the societal implications of AI by placing society in an immanent and unavoidable relationship with new technologies.

In terms of work, for example, the core of the argument is that there will be a rapid substitution of labour by AI. This potentially includes highly skilled professionals.

At Moomin, top management is engaging with new technologies and developing a dialogue in the ecosystem where smart and meaningful solutions are sought. Substituting human labour with AI is not the primary strategic challenge here. Rather, it is about recruiting technologically savvy people in all positions who share the Moomin ethos and values and are willing to contribute together to its success.

People are still needed to run the show. In scaling businesses, entrepreneurial management scholar Jeffrey Rayport encourages us to build a team of talented, highly motivated staff who believe in the company's mission. If you compromise on talent early, Rayport claims, it is harder to backtrack. Rayport was cited by Lauren Landry in her *Harvard Business School Online Business Insights Blog*.

Like many others, Rayport focuses on start-ups and growth firms and the first recruits in the venture. This first wave is made up of those who propagate the values of the organization and hire other performers ... who tend to be a lot like them.

In this way, grains of homosociality are built into these growing organizations. As human beings, we tend to seek and prefer the company of people who we consider similar to us in some significant way. Such homosociality can be framed as competence to legitimize choices and decisions, often referred to as 'fit' with the organization and its people and practices. This helps to explain why the same kinds of people tend to prevail in specific circumstances such as high-tech start-ups and growth firms.

The Moomin ecosystem has developed over the years, and it continues to develop. The people-related dynamics of engaging with new technologies are different from start-ups that are by definition starting from scratch. The ecosystem includes units that operate like start-ups, but talent is a relative and a broader notion for Moomin.

Scaling the digital footprint is a complex endeavour where all kinds of people with different and complementary capabilities are needed. There is no way single individuals can be on top of all things all the time. Designers collaborate with salespeople, data scientists collaborate with storytellers, coders collaborate with approvals experts, and so on. Everyone collaborates with everyone. And everything needs to be coordinated and managed, strategically even.

★★★

AI is predicted by technology experts to trigger a large-scale management revolution leading to radically improved organizational performance.

The underlying assumption is that the benefits of technologies can only be achieved if organizations transform their cultures and succeed in adopting a data-centric view where they abandon old practices such as reliance on human experience and intuition. It seems that the role that humans play in this disruption and transformation is, perhaps inadvertently, side-lined by the powerful technology narrative.

At Moomin, protecting the brand while letting it blossom means that people cannot be sidelined. Staying true to Tove Jansson's legacy means that people are needed, not only in making strategic decisions and choices, but also retaining the ethical compass in the business.

The Moomin strength of 'great content', as Erica Terranova put it, is crafted and produced by people who are mindful of the values of love, equality, and courage. At best, these are coded into the algorithms underpinning Moomin games, animations, and augmented realities. Technologies and technological solutions do not emerge out of thin air but are made by people. Keeping taps on the new technology partners is essential for Moomin, and an increasing risk.

There is mounting evidence of the potential dangers associated with the implementation of new technologies too quickly. It is challenging to integrate emerging technologies into existing work processes in organizations. This leads to discrepancies, tensions, friction, loss of time and money, and blame-games.

In the end, it is always humans who choose whether or not to abdicate their authority and to empower some piece of technology to intervene on their behalf. The accountability and responsibility, or ethical agency, lies with humans, despite the 'magic'.

Finally, in the era of new technologies, potential offered by physical and software automation robots is causing a stir. Robots carry out complex series of actions automatically and this is again an area with lots of hype. Rather than robots per se, our attention is directed to how humans and robots can work together in smart ways.

Home robots, among others, are predicted to proliferate in the future. For the Moomin business, this raises some interesting questions. How many of us would like to have a Moomin robot at home? Perhaps to just entertain us, to help us with our daily chores, or as an assistant that reminds us about our engagements? How about Moomin robots in hospitals and libraries?

All this sounds like an unusual scenario today, and the connections to Tove Jansson's art seem loose, to say the least. Yet, brainstorming about such possibilities is typical to technology discourse and hype, and it is always a part of the search for new solutions. There are no silly questions in these discussions.

Robots mimicking a lifelike appearance or automating movements convey a sense of intelligence. It is interesting to note how non-human entities such as robots are frequently attributed a human form, characteristics, and behaviour. This can be referred to as anthropomorphism, a tendency amplified by popular science fiction books and the movie industry that seeks to appeal to our imagination and capture our fantasies.

The tendency to anthropomorphize or humanize technologies makes it easier to convince us of their intelligence. However, akin to many other digital technologies, robots are developed and let loose in workplaces with high expectations but turn out to be more complicated than initially thought and promised.

Sometimes bots, or algorithms without physical or visual form, are referred to as robots in the workplace discourse. Organization and management scholar Katja Einola and colleagues studied anthropomorphizing these technological entities. Their analysis reveals a rift between managers who are excited and hopeful about the future capabilities of AI and employees who are frustrated and angry about its present shortcomings. Einola and colleagues argue that AI solutions influence the affective life of organizations and serve to amplify existing discontent between its members. Anthropomorphizing must be done with care.

No Moomin robots are to be expected any time soon. Moominizing robots, or making them Moomin-like or Moominous, is an attractive thought but not altogether realistic yet. Moomin robots may just be considered eerie by humans. Replacing humans in Moomin costumes with robots poses risks, to put it mildly.

Organization scholar Peter Fleming argues that robots have no volition (at least for now) and they are not 'motivated' to take humans' jobs. They are only as smart or stupid as people who designed them make them to be and depend on what people who co-exist with them decide to use them for.

Overall, the magic of technology should not be taken over the top. Businesses such as Moomin must be on the cutting edge of technology, but not too far too early. They must stay true to their values and develop their values base only gradually alongside, and with, new technologies.

Jeffrey Rayport argues that questions of speed and scope are essential in digitalizing and in entering virtual worlds. But how fast is too fast? How far is too far? Who decides? Why?

Perhaps the most significant technology-based initiative related to Moomin's strategic partnerships and licensees has only recently been developed. Thomas Zambra has been actively engaged in rolling out new software that makes it possible to put every Moomin image or object into a digital repository that allows licensees to sign-in and search for something they would like to put in their game, picture book, or on any (appropriate) physical product. This is developed in collaboration with Brainbase who offer 'One platform to unify your global licensing operations'.

This initiative is based on digitalizing, that is, making digital versions of Tove Jansson's work. Licensees send the Approvals Department at Moomin Characters their proposals and these are adjusted and corrected, and in most cases then approved. What seems to be particularly useful to the Moomin licensing business is that the licensees report the sales related to that licensed object through the same system, which then calculates the royalties based on the commission in the original licensing agreement.

Unifying licensing operations at Moomin by building and operating the digital repository is a huge effort to streamline something that is otherwise difficult to coordinate and manage comprehensively. Strategic partners and licensees get a better service while, yes, they are engaged in yet another way to scale Moomin's digital footprint – and to develop its brand.

★★★

In addition to high-profile initiatives such as collaboration with Rovio, the *Moominvalley* series, virtual worlds, and the unifying of licensing operations, new technologies impact on Moomin management in other, less glamorous but nevertheless significant ways. People and technologies operate together all the time in different online spaces.

New online spaces pop up and social media are a significant contemporary example of this. For Moomin, social media platforms are branding devices and distribution channels. "Because we mostly work with licensing, we also want to work with our fans. That's where social media management comes in," Thomas Zambra told us.

Social media platforms complement other channels and help reach people that would be difficult to reach otherwise. However, while consumers in a sense become unpaid co-producers of corporate brand value, as Dennis

K. Mumby among others suggests, social media are impossible to fully control and difficult to manage.

Social media refers to online communication platforms that allow users to create content and relate to content created by others. As spaces for activities that are social by nature, social media not only change the logic of human interaction online and offline but reshape power relations across platforms, media, users, and social institutions. People connect across time and space, based on assumed shared interests, and they can experience a sense of belonging that transcends geographical and other boundaries.

Moomin seem to regularly trigger social media activity in Finland. The Finnish Broadcasting Company YLE published some time ago a feature online article on how 'the Moomin craze filled up social media with joke mugs'. The article written by Anu Leena Koskinen recalled how people had cued overnight to purchase the new Moomin mug, how the limited edition was sold out immediately, and how mugs were then put on sale for huge prices online.

This led many Finns to design their own humorous mugs and to slap outrageous price tags on them. The article included a set of images of mugs on Twitter. Perhaps inevitably, some included Moomin characters in rude poses. People had their fun and moved on.

Overall, the distinction between producers and consumers of online content is muddled, and the ability to circulate becomes a key criterion of success for social media content.

As organization scholars Emma Bell and Pauline Leonard argue, achieving plausibility and verisimilitude is crucial. Social media communities assess the authority of the communicator against criteria such as authenticity. However, the truthfulness of information circulating in these communities is increasingly difficult to determine.

Texts and visuals also tend to be sharper, more intolerant, and more inflammatory online than in face-to-face interaction. Commenting on a given topic tends to unfold in gushes of emotional uproar or outrage – inviting people to react to each other's comments on the spur of the moment – before the commotion abruptly dies down and commenters move on to something else.

As management scholar Madeline Toubiana and Charlene Zietsma's study shows, social media are prone to 'echo chamber' effects in amplifying emotional reinforcement between like-minded people. The highly emotional nature of social media communication tends to polarize experiences and opinions between communities of people.

In fan communities across the world, different 'right' ways to be a Moomin fan are argued over, and these arguments spill over to how fans monitor the actions of the Moomin business ecosystem and how they (refuse to) purchase Moomin items.

When fans get active on social media, they take the Moomin brand in all sorts of directions. As social media are characterized by fast paced exchanges, many of these efforts will never reach the eyes and ears of Moomin decision-makers, despite sophisticated data tracking.

Sometimes they do, as the 'boat Moomin' incident discussed in Chapter 3 showed us. Some form of managerial action was immediately required. As we saw, however, the comments and discussions meandered in all sorts of directions. Typically for social media, though, the commotion was short lived.

The 'boat Moomin' incident demonstrates another key feature of online spaces that impacts upon the dynamics of interaction. People can verbally and visually build on their own and each other's digital traces online. Digital traces remain; they are still there in one form or another, ready to be retrieved.

Traces of old incidents can suddenly appear in new forms elsewhere, interpreted and framed differently, and with new meanings and associations. Based on their research, language scholar Heike Baldauf and her colleagues call these traces 'mirrors with memory'.

Traces come in all shapes and sizes. For example, there are all sorts of Moomin videos around. YouTube is the global online video sharing and social media platform owned by Google. A Google search of the words 'Moomin' and 'YouTube' returns millions of hits. This includes official Moomin videos of various kinds and videos by Moomin licensees.

Self-made videos by fans and others featuring Moomin characters and merchandise are also widely represented on YouTube. Some of these are dubious, to say the least, from the viewpoint of the Moomin brand.

We cannot expect the principle of generosity to stretch to these spaces. Online videos remain in many ways out of reach from the viewpoint of Moomin management. And, of course, given that Moomin or Mumin is a male first name popular in Muslim faith, meaning 'believer' in Arabic, not all the millions of Google hits concern Tove Jansson's creations.

In 2019, online children's network and studio WildBrain, owned by DHX Media, was hired to develop a global YouTube strategy for Moomin. WildBrain was tapped by Gutsy Animations to manage Moomin-related content and to develop the strategy for the animation series *Moominvalley*. This included behind-the-scenes material and other content created exclusively for YouTube.

Like all online and offline spaces, social media communities have their celebrated stars. Social media influencers help steer opinion. These are people who have built a reputation for their (assumed) knowledge and expertise on a specific topic. Influencer marketing is a form of social media marketing involving endorsements and product placement on influencers' social media channels and sites.

Tiina Liukkonen, Chief Communications Officer at All Things Commerce, told us that working with influencers is expensive and that it requires both resources and substance know-how. However, "it can be the most effective way of marketing nowadays when the fit is great, as it's considered so genuine. Many people make their purchasing decisions based on influencers nowadays, compared to traditional lifestyle magazines, for example."

"Other positive benefits of working with influencers is exposing the brand to new demographics, increase diverse representation, and spread the values that Moomin stories are based on," Tiina added.

Moomin has turned attention to micro-influencers who are people with a social media following larger than an average person's but smaller than that of a celebrity. Micro-influencers use their following to promote products relevant to their interests or expertise. According to Tiina, All Things Commerce has been "experimenting with micro-influencers" who are engaging with different topics and specializing in different fields.

As an art- and values-based brand, Moomin is active in producing 'great content' and in engaging with fans on social media. However, relying only on social media is not recommended. Erica Terranova from the marketing team at All Things Commerce wrote in her blog on seobuddy.com: 'At Moomins, we strongly believe in email marketing and work extensively on growing our Fanclub members and provide them with great content via email.'

Having a loyal fanbase is essential for the Moomin business. Staying in touch with those fans who are interested in sharing Moomin content is a great asset. Social media influencers add to this mix by drawing people's attention to all things Moomin – thus further (re)creating the Moomin brand.

The Moomin business success story has caught the interest of many actors active in digital worlds. Podcasts or digital audio files that a user can download to a personal device to listen to are increasingly popular. Stockholm-based Soundtelling is an audio content company that makes original podcasts, branded storytelling, and other audio content. At the time of our ethnographic study, they engaged in making sense of Moomin and its success in their podcasts.

We observed the first briefing meeting Soundtelling had with key actors at Moomin. Thomas Zambra and others recited the Moomin story and what has made the business ecosystem possible. "Tove's original books are the source of everything else," Thomas said. "There are new interpretations of Moomin, in part because there are changes in visual technology that requires some adjustment."

Reciting the Moomin ethos, Thomas added: "With the podcast we want to succeed in creating something that is so interesting that it goes out and over any commercial thinking so that people start to talk about it. We want the podcast to captivate listeners." Nanette Forsström, Producer at Moomin Characters, added that "I think we would like to have something that can reach a global audience. And that it would also raise people's expectations for us."

Johanna Stenback, Managing Director of All Things Content, summarized the intended experience of listening to the Moomin podcasts: "Inclusion. That anyone who listens to it feels included in what they hear. There should be surprises. Insights. Know-how. Empathy. And humour. And I think that we should direct ourselves to a kind of thinking person who has a breadth of knowledge or thirst for knowledge."

Digitalizing generously

Engaging with new technologies can be understood to be a major strategic change or transformation initiative at Moomin, akin to focusing the brand on Tove Jansson's art since 2008. Digitalization overall has been more incremental and a little less deliberate process than the strategic rebranding exercise. Exploration and execution – the cornerstones of strategy work at Moomin – have been key aspects of Moomin entering virtual digitalized spaces.

Investments have been made and the infrastructure is beginning to be in place. We will learn in due course how the investments pay off, how the infrastructure functions and is further developed, and how it affects growth and profitability.

Expanding into digital and virtual worlds, into the unknown, has already yielded key business learnings for Moomin management. It is advisable to do it with purpose and sufficiently big, rather than to consider a simple add-on to existing operations. Expanding into digital and virtual worlds entails new forms of strategic partnerships, which must be meticulously managed for any discrepancies in how key Moomin values are enacted.

In terms of consumers, it is not only about digitalizing but engaging with online media and their logics. Expanding into digital and virtual worlds is, ultimately, about plausibility and authenticity – staying true to the roots – and negotiations with new stakeholders so that authenticity can be retained. For Moomin, this relates to Tove Jansson's legacy, and the values drawn from it.

The digital realm allows a broader discourse about companies and greater opportunities for consumers to engage with their products and services. One interesting example is the field of video games, based on the books and movies of fiction writers.

In a study of video game adaptations of J.R.R. Tolkien's *The Lord of the Rings*, Mark Rowell Wallin proposes that game-makers must balance between fidelity to the original story so that it is recognizable as such, and innovation in terms of new possibilities so that their game stands out from competitors. Wallin points out that the game's purpose is not to reproduce the story but to enter the world in which the stories take place – opening up the possibility to experience that world in new ways.

In the case of Moomins, video games are not so much about a specific plot created by Tove Jansson, but about being in the Moominvalley, with the characters. The same holds true for adaptations of other fantasy works, such as the Chronicles of Narnia, the Land of Oz, or Harry Potter.

★★★

How does generosity play into all this? Generosity works through people, as Erica Terranova's example noted earlier shows us. 'Great content' created by people for people is the grounding on which the Moomin digital footprint is extended. Generosity in virtual worlds and online spaces is in this sense not much different from generosity in branding in general or in doing strategy generously. It is grounded in the Moomin values.

In her study of altruism online, media psychologist Dana Klisanin pointed to how digitalization allows people to participate in various ways to change the world. From 'click-to-donate' at one end of the scale to multi-party global platforms organizing volunteers and activists at the other end, the digital world can give us new ways to be generous.

Nevertheless, the fact that generosity is entangled in the functionalities of technologies steers the forms it takes in online spaces. Social media platforms are fundamentally technological, and their technologies differ. Specific functionalities of technologies determine what can and cannot be done – and this applies to generosity too.

Looking at the early rise of social media, marketing scholars Patrick Barwise and Sean Meehan noted that 'as usual, marketers are turning hype into hyperventilation'. They advised against rewriting the marketing playbook in the face of apparently dramatic changes. Instead, activities and initiatives in social media amplified the need to get the basics right.

Barwise and Meehan reminded us that a great brand always offers a clear and relevant promise for clients, builds trust by delivering on the promise, drives the market by continually improving on it, and seeks further advantage by innovating beyond the familiar. In all the turmoil, they argued, you must keep an eye on those fundamentals.

Revise your playbook, rather than rewrite it, was Barwise and Meehan's advice: continue to focus on delivering your brand promise in the constantly changing conditions.

Today, the playbook is not only revised but rewritten, at least to some extent, although branding is still about getting the basics right. Moomin engages with social media functionalities and tries to manage their affordances, as Tiina Liukkonen earlier explained.

Adapting psychology scholar James J. Gibson's ideas on affordance, it can be understood to relate to how a property of an object such as social media platform defines its possible uses or makes clear how it can (not) or should (not) be used. Affordances of texts, visual images, and their combinations on different social media platforms shape possibilities for action. They signify the enabling and constraining potential for meaning-making offered by verbal and visual resources for Moomin today.

Affordances steer possible associations, temporalities, editability, storytelling, and so on. The passion that is characteristic of engaging with Moomin takes different forms on different social media platforms and offers different opportunities and threats for generosity.

While Twitter (now X) has first and foremost been about short sharp textual messages, Instagram is about visuality and visual branding. Facebook is a social networking platform that has been argued to be in relative decline in recent years. Branded hashtags such as #moomin, #moomins, #moominmug or #tovejansson are important for engaging with these platforms and others. Including these in social media communications offers easy ways for followers to search for Moomin across platforms. They help collect all relevant social content in specific places.

Thinking through affordances and what is (not) possible is crucial in digital spaces. Twitter (latterly renamed X), Instagram, and Facebook all prioritize content that gets shared. Moomin social media experts told us that they are focusing on timely content that incentivizes sharing. In recent years, Moomin has become active in TikTok, embracing its logic of short and shareable moving visual content.

The different functionalities of social media platforms, however, allow for incentivizing sharing in different ways. At the time of writing this book, we were told that online ads in the right places were the fastest way to reach a lot of people. The top Moomin online ad at the time of our study had reached 3,2 million people.

While embracing the possibilities of technologies, generosity is about acknowledging that technologies are not neutral. In her book *Weapons of Math Destruction*, Cathy O'Neil offered a critical take on the societal impact of algorithms or sets of instructions for conducting sequences of specified actions coded in computer programs. These increasingly steer our lives. O'Neil is a mathematician and data scientist who explored how algorithms are increasingly used in ways that reinforce pre-existing inequalities in societies and organizations.

There is a distinct risk that inequalities based on gender, race or ethnicity, and social class are not only reproduced but intensified in digital and virtual worlds. Coders code their own biases into the algorithms, which then do what algorithms do: spread and multiply the biases endlessly. Cathy O'Neil warned us against being naïve in engaging with algorithms.

Moomin management seems to be aware of the pitfalls of new technologies. Digitalizing generously is a trial-and-error process where the coherence of the Moomin story is tested time and again. With new kinds of strategic partners (whose purpose and values are sometimes difficult to detect) Moomin must be extra careful in defending Tove Jansson's legacy and ideals.

Figure 6.1: Moomins enjoying life

Source: © Moomin Characters™

At the same time, the Moomin purpose of doing business *and* doing good has come to life in new ways. The campaign to save the Baltic Sea from pollution, referred to in Chapter 4, was technologically mediated. Most of the actions took place online under the banner of #OURSEA. The hashtag led people to the right places and campaign products were purchased, and money was donated, through the website.

While digitalizing generously is an increasingly important issue for Moomin, we keep coming back to people. We have saved what we think is the most important element in the Moomin ecosystem for last. Next, we explore how people are managed at Moomin and consider what it means to manage people generously.

7

People: It Is Alright to Be Broken

"For me, it is all about love and friendship. People are taken care of here, and you can be yourself. I can tell my stupid jokes and laugh and be silly," Marina Lindström told us. Marina works as Producer at Moomin Characters. She is as excited about her work as the day when she first started several years ago.

"If you work hard, you must have fun. I wouldn't do it if I didn't enjoy it so much. I have gone through some bad experiences in my life, and Moomin has always been there to support me." Marina's comments suggest that people management at Moomin is something special.

'The Moomin stories are adored by adults as much as they are by children largely for the range of life lessons and philosophies to be found in Moominvalley', the Moomin Group onboarding booklet for new employees claims. 'From the importance of respecting people even if you disagree with them, to how to tell whether or not someone is dangerous by how much they like to eat pancakes and jam, there is wisdom to be found on every page and from every inhabitant, large or small.'

The onboarding booklet recites the Moomin values of love, equality, and courage. We are told that Tove Jansson's Moomins follow these values 'to live in happiness and harmony with their diverse group of friends and acquaintances'. All Moomin employees, old and new, are invited to join in and make the leap from fiction to their work and lives. The onboarding booklet takes people by the hand and lets them know what this could mean. Yet, these materials only tell so much, and the reality is more complicated.

"Some people say that you can't be married to your work, but I love my work and I love my colleagues," Marina Lindström told us with a smile. "It's more than work. It's like the Moominhouse where everyone is taken care of and respected and welcomed. There are also some disagreements, but it's just a special atmosphere here, that you don't find elsewhere."

Marina is talking about the human side of management. This is a tricky conceptual terrain. It is difficult to understand management without humans, but sometimes people management as a concept is reserved for specialists dedicated to the task.

While people management (some call it human resources management or HRM) is typically a staff function in organizations, professionals who do this work have always fought to uplift its strategic role. They coordinate recruitment, talent management, and leadership development, for example, and try to find ways to work with line management, or people in business functions who have direct responsibility for others.

Dave Ulrich has been one of the most influential scholars and consultants in the field of HRM and people management. His thinking has shifted from viewing human resource roles, competences, value propositions and transformation to turning the concept of human resources (HR) around and understanding it from the outside-in, through the value it can bring to the customer interface in organizations.

Those who are engaged with HR or people management tend to juggle between people and numbers. Convincing top management about why people matter has proven to be surprisingly difficult. Perhaps paradoxically, it is often best done with numbers.

At Moomin, people management is understood generously and there is no designated HR function. So, at Moomin, it concerns everyone, inside-out and outside-in. It casts leadership and diversity, to name a few examples of popular concepts associated with people management, in a specific light.

In this chapter, we zoom in on how people are managed in the Moomin ecosystem. In the end, it is the organization and its people (and people and technologies together) that determine what is possible to do. Success or failure is not about individuals, not even the gutsiest decision-makers or the most ardent rebels. It is about doing things together – or failing to do them.

This is why the Moomin organization and ecosystem as a social community is crucial for making sense of the prospects of its business and the plausibility and authenticity of the Moomin brand.

Managing people at Moomin is grounded in storytelling about Tove Jansson, the Moomins, and their wisdom. Storytelling is used in branding, building strategic partnerships, engaging people in strategy work, and making use of new technologies. How people in the ecosystem adopt the story and engage with it (or fail to do so), making it their own (or abandoning it), is a question of life and death for the Moomin business ecosystem.

This is where generosity once again enters the scene. Generosity is always faced with difficult people-related questions. Our attention thus turns to managing differences and developing a resilient organization, face to face as well as virtually. We also consider how broken people – those who are hurt or have problems – are supported in the Moomin ecosystem. After all, it is how those in the most vulnerable positions are treated that determines the plausibility of the generous Moomin brand in practice.

Members of the resilient organization unite!

'It is important to note that this is the result of a conscious, years-long choice to focus on content production above all else', Erica Terranova from the marketing team at All Things Commerce described branding at Moomin in a guest blog article for seobuddy.com. She added that its success is 'thanks to the effort of the whole company in building a reputable, beloved brand and bring the Moomins successfully to the digital sphere'. Like Marina Lindström's message, Erica's was equally clear: Moomin is special, even in digital and virtual worlds.

In the short biography accompanying her blog, Erica Terranova was presented as 'an academic turned marketer who started doing marketing because she needs to keep learning new things to be happy'. Having worked with business-to-business software as service and in a hypergrowth tech startup, Erica was now 'at Moomins, where she focuses on growth marketing, performance marketing, and e-commerce optimization. Working for such a beloved cultural powerhouse has been incredibly fulfilling, as it allows Erica to promote values she strongly believes in and help make the world a kinder place.'

Marina Lindström, in turn, has a background in project management in advertising and as a producer in a design agency. Marina and her team work closely with CEO Roleff Kråkström, serving Moomin strategic partners and licensees. "Like in the Moominhouse, people need to feel welcome," Marina said. "When we have a meeting, I want people to come here and feel good. We want to send this message to all our clients and partners."

Marina summarized how she is managed at Moomin: "Rolle would never say, 'I'm your boss!' and just tell me what to do without me being able to state my opinion. We are all equal here." Marina told us that she also works closely with her team: "In other companies, there can be this competitive thing against your colleagues and back-stabbing, but not here. I can say to my colleagues, 'I need help', and they are there for me, and I'm there for them. That's something to cherish."

During our ethnographic study it became clear to us that there is something about Moomin that attracts creative and socially conscious people who want to do good things and to develop as professionals.

Erica Terranova told us that she was "the first real foreigner" ever hired when she joined the Moomin Group in 2021. She is from Italy, and although there are other non-Finns on the staff, she was the first from outside northern Europe. Erica Terranova was passionate about breaking barriers and about learning, and she was outspoken about how to make things better for all.

Keeping the likes of Marina Lindström and Erica Terranova happy and productive is what people management at Moomin is about. Love, equality, and courage are likely to mean different things for different people, or at least the emphasis on what can be done in the name of these values varies. These differences must – and can – be managed with generosity. Securing a sufficiently shared understanding of the key Moomin values is thus of paramount importance. How people are managed – and how they are encouraged to manage themselves – contributes to branding, partnerships, strategy, and digitalization.

There is no business, brand, or strategy without shared understandings and ways of doing things that bind people together. And people are strange. They seldom do exactly as they are told. They grumble. Sometimes they resist outright or just ignore the fantastic strategic schemes and initiatives that are developed for them. The key word – and the source of the challenge – is 'for'. People tend to be put off when something is done 'for' them.

At Moomin, the key principle is 'with'. Doing branding, partnerships, strategy, and technology with people is a key element in the success of the Moomin ecosystem. Managing people is about giving them opportunities to show what they can do, viewing mistakes and failure as sources of joint learning, and celebrating achievements together. These principles may sound cheesy, but we found them to be a natural part of the functioning of the Moomin ecosystem.

We could talk about leadership here but decided against it. Leadership is a fluffy notion and difficult to take apart from management anyway. Leadership is often defined as influencing and guiding people – and distinguished from the management of 'things'. Leadership is associated with leaders or individuals who by virtue of their position or capabilities are expected to lead others.

Critical organization scholars Mats Alvesson and Stefan Sveningsson studied leadership as what they call the 'extra-ordinarization of the mundane'. This is an intriguing notion because it cuts to the core of the leadership concept and exposes its fluffiness and hype. Rather than certain acts such as listening to people and chatting with them being significant in themselves, Alvesson and Sveningsson argue, it is their being done by managers that gives them a special, emotional value beyond their everyday significance. These mundane things become leadership when they are done by people who are designated leaders.

At the same time, critical leadership studies tell us that individualistic notions of leadership too often lead to hero worship. Like Moomin, we as authors of this book steer clear of upbeat and naïve celebrations of corporate heroes. We refuse to offer simplified advice for becoming generous managers or leaders.

Leadership development scholar Rakesh Khurana's research showed that heroes and 'superstar' managers tend to leave more confusion and even destruction in their wake than long-term success. Yet people inadvertently end up celebrating exceptional qualities of inspirational and charismatic leaders when they talk about leadership.

"We are very much against heroes, as Tove Jansson was," Roleff Kråkström told us. While Roleff himself is an active and visible figure in the Moomin ecosystem, he seems to make sure that he does not push himself forward to take credit from others. Instead, Roleff takes on the role of (elderly) statesman who is part of a community: "I have no intention to be a star. The focus is on the brand and the values."

If we did talk about leaders and leadership, we would do it following Ikujiro Nonaka and Hirotaka Takeuchi's ideas. They were founding fathers of the concept of knowledge management. Nonaka and Takeuchi argue for wise leaders who create the future by pursuing the common good and whose thinking extends beyond the company. This is about being in tune with tacit as well as explicit knowledge in making decisions that allows the company to live in harmony with society. However, leaders must also draw on practical wisdom. Nonaka and Takeuchi suggest that this can only be acquired through experience.

Nonaka and Takeuchi argue that wise leaders help their companies to start thinking of themselves as social entities charged with a mission to create lasting benefits for society. According to Nonaka and Takeuchi, wise leaders make judgements knowing that everything is contextual, make decisions knowing that everything is changing, and take actions knowing that everything depends on doing so in a timely fashion.

Nonaka and Takeuchi's ideas on wisdom are a far cry from the Western individualistic hero worship that is characteristic of a lot of popular leadership literature. Their arguments about wisdom strike us as something related to generosity.

Yet, the concept of leadership is not directly useful here. People and 'things' are intertwined in practice, and it is seldom smart to keep them apart. Moreover, Moomin management is about different people doing things together, rather than lone efforts of heroic individual leaders.

Roleff said with a smile: "I'm sure that Tom and James Zambra and others think of me as some sort of boomer. But it's just great to see different generations and people of all ages working together."

Our focus turns to joint activities rather than lone heroes. Like with the idea of viewing strategy as doing, managing people is about recurring activities and practices and consistency. It is something very mundane and unglamorous: keeping the mill running from one day to the next.

★★★

For managing people meaningfully, an understanding of why the organization functions the way it does is needed; what its history is, what are the people-related dynamics that allow it to develop and prosper – and, at the same time, what are the potential sources of hindrances to progress.

At Moomin, as we have seen in the previous chapters, there is an exceptionally clear idea of what the organization is and what it stands for. All the way from the story of ideas, from the life and work of Tove Jansson, there seems to be a 'red thread' running through the art and business. Because the Moomin story and values are continuously repeated, discussed, and reflected upon, they serve as a natural grounding for people management.

While repetition can be boring, it is nevertheless an essential part of how people learn. When the story is as strong as it is at Moomin, repetition makes sense. Through repeating it in ways that ever so slightly help reinterpret and tweak the story over time, a sense of purpose and sense of direction can be established, and the organization is steered so that it gradually changes form, as we found in the chapters on strategy work and technologies.

All too often top managers – people who like to think of themselves as strategists – complain about what they think are communication problems in implementing strategy. They say that they have established a great strategy but have failed to communicate it to others in the organization. This is the excuse given for why the organization does not execute the planned strategy.

However, the real issue may not be communication per se, but how strategy is done. As a rule, people do not like to be on the receiving end of communication. They do not like surprises. They prefer to be involved in preparing stuff right from the start and to have their say in things that they think matter; they like coherence and clarity; and, at least in Nordic societies such as Finland, fairness and a sense of equality too.

More specifically, people like to think that they have a chance to be heard, if they so desire. They do not necessarily want to exercise that right. One way or the other, it is always nice to know that someone will listen if you feel like saying something. Communication, then, is just the tip of the iceberg.

At Moomin, repeating Tove Jansson's legacy – and the brand that binds everything together – serves to keep up coherence, clarity, and a sense of fairness. However, people are not only strange. They are different. Some like to actively join in, others to look from afar, or to question things.

We witnessed how many are passionate about their work and engagement with Moomin, but not all, at least not all the time. Managing differences takes a multitude of forms and it is a crucial part of people management.

"We have many socially awkward people here. This includes me," Roleff Kråkström explained to us with a smile. "We are a bunch of creatively paranoid optimists, all in our different ways. We first spur each other to consider that everything is wrong. We then find solutions together and make things happen."

Whereas Roleff likes to downplay his own role in the Moomin ecosystem, others elevate his significance in making the system work. His persona, as seen by others, is dynamic and charismatic. In terms of generosity, and as discussed previously, this is a distinct risk for Moomin. Should Roleff step down, the story must nevertheless continue, and he is very much aware of this. This leads us to managing differences, which is another crucial aspect of people management at Moomin. We could have used popular terms such as diversity and inclusion to discuss difference(s) at Moomin but decided not to.

Critical studies by organization scholar Patrizia Zanoni and colleagues, among others, show that diversity is an artificial concept. There is no absolute universal definition of diversity, just human beings with their different appearances, characteristics, and idea(l)s. We are a little put off by the concept of diversity because it can be used for window dressing and masking inequalities behind the façade of happy faces and box-ticking exercises.

The problem is that diversity is not only artificial. Diversity scholar and consultant Jonna Louvrier's research shows how the diverse are typically viewed in a frame of 'lack' as they fail to meet the organizational norm. Those who are seen as diverse lack something essentially important due to, for example, their gender or colour of skin. As such, diversity does not challenge norms in organizations, but casts those who do not fit the dominant norms as deviant, deficient, and diverse, and in need of special support.

So, no fancy diversity talk. In line with the Moomin value of equality, we ground our understanding on differences and why they matter. At Moomin, everyone is different, and this includes high-profile decision-makers such as Sophia Jansson and Roleff Kråkström.

Organizational 'norms' are multifaceted, not a bunch of people who all think, act, and look the same. Like in the Moominvalley, however, respecting difference comes with some edge. It is not only about happy faces and smiles, but disagreements and arguments too.

"We have reached a stage where we actually thrive on tensions and conflicts and on solving them. We have 'fights' regularly," Roleff argued, gesticulating with his fingers. "This is one aspect of our sometimes brutally honest way to relate to each other. We don't bullshit each other, and we don't let people second-guess. We build on our differences and different opinions."

There are differences in how people adapt (or fail to adapt) the Moomin story and engage with it, making it their own (or abandoning it). Moomin is not a cult where people are brainwashed to think and act alike. On the contrary, like in the Moominvalley, rebels are part of the fabric, and they blend into the community. Different viewpoints and arguments are appreciated as sources of potentially innovative solutions and learning.

In some ways, Erica Terranova appeared to be a rebel at Moomin. She was outspoken about her views on how the Moomin brand should be developed in the spirit of Tove Jansson. For example, Erica stressed the importance of including images of different kinds of people in Moomin materials. She argued for how important it is that children and adults with different skin colours can associate themselves with the Moomins and life in the Moominvalley.

Why the colour of someone's skin should matter in branding may not be immediately understandable to many white Finns who have grown up in a society that has only in recent decades opened for immigration and cultural and ethnic blending. Finland is changing and Moomin is changing in this respect too. Perhaps someone from the outside is needed to show how and why ethnicity and race matter for all businesses, including Moomin.

Of course, who is a rebel and who is not will always be a relative notion. Some people may have joined a company in the Moomin ecosystem as an act of rebellion against established players in their respective business. The publishing company Förlaget, for example, has attracted people who feel strongly about promoting Swedish language literature from Finland and about increasing literary diversity. This can be thought of as a form of rebellion.

How people are managed at Moomin offers interesting angles to organizational practices such as recruitment, talent management, and performance management. Moomin have their own ways of recruiting people, and they are not keen on managing talent in a structured way or breathing down people's necks in the name of monitoring their performance.

"Moomin Characters was my customer, and Roleff called and asked me if I wanted to join in. We were nine or ten people when I started," Marina Lindström recalled her way into the Moomin ecosystem. "The office manager had her beloved paper calendar when I first came here. My colleagues and I managed to convince her to put a Google calendar in place," Marina laughed and continued:

'There was little structure back then. This is interesting from a project coordination perspective. But we have come a long way, and, for example, Thomas Zambra and other younger colleagues are bringing in more systems, which is great. I wonder whether he knows the office was on a paper calendar less than ten years ago?'

Roleff Kråkström added with a smile that he takes pride in having migrated to a fully digital version immediately when mobile phones allowed for it. "I originally disliked the idea of sharing my calendar but quickly got my head around it. Now I can't grasp how we ever managed without it."

The curious thing is that the Moomin Group has no traditional HR function through which key practices such as recruitment and talent management are typically organized in companies. Recruitment refers to processes of identifying, sourcing, screening, shortlisting, and interviewing candidates for jobs. When new people are recruited to Moomin, those directly concerned organize the process and make the decisions.

There are two sides to every coin. Based on her own experiences, Growth Marketing Lead Erica Terranova shared her ideas on how to improve one's chances of getting hired. She stressed the importance of understanding the company and their problems, and on offering a compelling case "on why you are uniquely qualified to solve their problem and what are your strategy ideas and plans for the role". If you really want a job, Erica said, going the extra mile is important: "Show, don't tell how good you are."

And once you get the job, Erica argued, "never stop learning. It is important to always invest in your professional development and keep networking, support organizations you believe in, and be involved in your professional community."

After they are recruited and when they have settled in, people's potential needs to be assessed, or that is how it is usually thought of. Talent management is typically a part of HR work in companies. It is about anticipating the required 'human capital' and planning how to meet those needs, and it materializes as a set of practices to identify, attract, develop, and engage those individuals in the organization who are for some reason considered to be of specific value to it. This may be through their (assumed) high potential or because they fulfil critical organizational roles.

There is no talent management at Moomin. "What you see is what you get," Roleff Kråkström told us. "We recruit people for what they can do and what they are really good at. We don't promise them career opportunities." Roleff continued:

'This is a family company, and the top jobs are likely to be filled by family members anyway. And we don't let people create all sorts of fancy titles for themselves. They get a chance to proudly do what they love and to work with people who are equally committed and involved. We all learn from each other.'

Respect for differences is an integral part of Tove Jansson's work and the Moomin brand. Everyone is different, and everyone is accepted as they are. Apart from attitudes and mindsets, there are also differences in people's capabilities to deliver what they are expected to deliver.

In companies this is typically talked about as performance management, that is, how people's work is monitored and evaluated. At Moomin, people are not encouraged to track each other and each other's work.

In fact, performance management seems to be something of an anathema to Moomin. Key decision-makers at Moomin Characters do not want to set someone up as a supervisor whose job would be to monitor and evaluate other people working at what is important. This requires that the people who do the work love what they do and would do it with or without Moomin Characters in place. A good example is Maria Andersin, who was newly responsible for the Moomin archive at the time of our study. Maria was hired for skills that no-one else at Moomin had. Before joining Moomin, she had had a long career, from being a museum assistant to becoming director at the historical Lotta Svärd Museum located in Tuusula, near Helsinki in Finland. Maria was organizing – and literally cleaning up – the Moomin archive, and she was allowed to do what she thought best.

A few days before starting at Moomin Characters, Maria told us:

'The question that interests me is what do they want me to do? I don't know what they want me to prioritize. And that's something I must start with, look at what we have here in the archive and then ask them. What is important? Where do you want me to start? And for what purpose do you want me to do this?'

Maria was puzzled, because "normally in museum work, your boundaries are set beforehand. The decisions are a mirror of what is important in that moment, but we don't know what will be important in five years. Do we just look at what Tove Jansson produced? Or what Moomin Characters is producing today?"

Maria set to work defining the scope of Moomin Characters' archive, for example, distinguishing what is an 'artifact' and what is 'merchandise'. From there, she requested several different types of storage as Tove's original drawings could be on delicate paper requiring certain temperatures and humidity levels, and original paintings would require another level. One of the first things Maria did was to make sure that anyone touching the sensitive pieces was wearing cotton gloves.

How could Maria Andersin's performance be monitored and evaluated in the traditional way? Her mandate in the Moomin ecosystem was so unique and her tasks so wide and varied, that no performance management system could ever do justice to her valuable contributions. And there are many people like Maria at Moomin – most employees, perhaps.

The principle behind Moomin people management is to hire competence for a specific purpose and then embrace the risk that they might not do what they committed to. There is a way of managing risk through relationships rather than through control mechanisms. When people embrace the Moomin principles of openness and sharing in their work, the community around them are able to do (at least some of) the controlling.

We talked to Maria Andersin again after she had worked for Moomin for two years. She laughed, and said: "My comments actually look quite funny now." Maria told us that she solved the job description issue herself by crafting a "rather detailed Collection Policy Programme", which she presented to Roleff Kråkström who approved it.

Maria made sure she kept others in the organization in the loop by presenting the main points of her programme in the Moomin Characters monthly meeting. "After my presentation I have been working according to the programme, so I guess I'm kind of monitoring myself," Maria laughed. "This is my dream job, really!"

Maria's job description is evolving. Two years after our first interview with her, Maria said that:

'apart from working with the archive – safety, cataloguing, sorting, and so forth – I help our own team as well as external researchers to find sources and material for their work, and I assist with curation of exhibitions both in-house and externally. I just got back from closing an exhibition in Paris.'

Maria also reflected on the monthly meetings as a practice through which organizational members get to know what everyone else is up to. "Preparing for your presentations helps you to reflect on what you have done, what is on your table right now, and what should be prioritized," Maria told us. "The other teams and the management, too, get an overall idea of the activities in the company."

She concluded: "I wish to add that I've never got the feeling that the management is supervising me. The management, too, reports on how the company is doing in these meetings. Being informed makes us as employees feel that we are an important part of the ecosystem."

★★★

Nevertheless, no organization is without conflicts. An actor in the Moomin ecosystem told us about some of the tensions between the "upstairs and downstairs" people, referring to different companies located on different floors.

This person wished for a more "articulated strategy" overall for the ecosystem and its different parts, because at times there was a tendency to "hide behind the excuse that 'I don't know the priorities, so I didn't do this or that'." The message was that "we need to be even clearer about our priorities".

Yes, 'we'. The sense of community that is embraced at Moomin may seem to be at odds with some of the contemporary corporate ideals. Emphasis on new technologies today, for example, involves a discourse where exceptional individuals are celebrated. Jeffrey Rayport's ideas on scaling businesses include a lot of talk about high performers who are multiple times more productive than others. 'Cream of the crop A+ players can get the work done', according to Rayport.

At Moomin, this elitist discourse is not only redundant but actively avoided. The focus is on people's complementary capabilities and teamwork, on the 'we' rather than the 'I' or 'you'. Performance management, to the extent that it exists, is based on focus areas and goals. The key performance indicators (KPIs) in place relate to these areas and goals, and they are collective, not individual.

Taking care of employees takes many forms. Moomin Characters has set up a fund that is owned and managed by the personnel. As the employer, Moomin contributes to the capital as part of its renumeration policy. This is a collective form of financial incentive, and very much in the generous Moomin spirit.

Physical location and facilities also matter for people management in the name of love, equality, and courage. Nanette Forsström, Producer at Moomin Characters, shared her reflections on the Moomin open office design and the dynamics of interaction that it enables. There is little privacy at the office and in principle everyone gets to see and hear everything.

Because the CEO sits in the open office and takes calls from his desk, employees hear him make deals, negotiate, and proselytize new potential partners. There is an exercise of trust in that you have heard everything, and that the management have nothing to hide.

The Moomin brand and values such as love, equality, and courage make promises and raise expectations, and put a lot of pressure on delivering good people management. Like in George Orwell's allegorical novel *Animal Farm*, it may well be that all are equal, but some are more equal than others.

It is all beginning to sound perhaps suspiciously positive. Apart from "a tendency to speak about people behind their backs", as one employee put it, we encountered very little criticism of how people are treated at Moomin. Yet, every challenge must be tackled.

This employee went on to say about talking behind's people's backs that "you need to be on the top of your game so that you maintain your position. I know I am not alone because someone told me that 'This is not so nice, but you should know this!'" This aspect of how people relate to each other at Moomin needs to be voiced and dealt with, because "it is a kind of threat ... and if we don't stop it then we are part of the problem".

★★★

With these thoughts, we are back to the Moomin story and brand. The story needs to be plausible, coherent, and dynamic enough in everyone's eyes so that it spurs the right thoughts and actions. People need to see connections between the story and how they are treated. The story needs to feel real.

Choosing the right people to join the organization is the first step. The second step is to help people grow into something that they are comfortable with and find meaningful. All along, people need to be excited about their work – and about who they work for, and work with.

Roleff Kråkström told us: "We are a verbal organization. We are verbal both in working with the Moomin brand and in how we relate to each other as employees. This is another example of how branding and managing people are connected at Moomin. These are two sides of the same coin."

Storytelling is eternal in this kind of people management. Projections of possible futures are affected by both past and present events, and these events can always be interpreted in multiple ways. How people engage with stories and their temporalities varies and changes.

Drawing from the past always needs to make sense in the present. Too much leaning in the future can backfire. People at Moomin have their feet firmly on the ground while their heads are in the clouds. This is what we learned about strategy work in the ecosystem.

The mix of purpose and hands-on actions seems to frame everything that is done at Moomin, including people management. We are reminded here about the lack of explicit and detailed strategy talk in the ecosystem. With a clear sense of purpose and direction, and keeping eyes on exploration and execution, the organization and its people retain a shared sense of coherence while developing and changing flexibly over time.

★★★

Strategy and innovation scholars Gary Hamel and Liisa Välikangas introduced the notion of resilience to describe organizations that have developed shared capabilities that enable them to reinvent their business and strategy dynamically as circumstances change.

Strategic resilience refers to the capacity for continuous reconstruction and anticipating as well as adjusting to changes. Resilience seems like a useful concept to make sense of the Moomin ecosystem and its people. A resilient organization builds on foundations of strong uniting features (some call this culture, but we stick to purpose, values, and brand) and changes and develops continuously as markets and circumstances change.

Our research on the Moomin ecosystem suggests that it demonstrates resilience as it is characterized by shared capabilities not only in making quick decisions but also executing them fast. Scaling the digital footprint is one example of this.

Hamel and Välikangas assert that resilience means changing before the need to change becomes desperately obvious, that is, changing before you need a superstar hero to initiate a dramatic (and usually unsuccessful) transformation. Moomin's recent investments in technology-related initiatives, based on shared learning and development of capabilities, help the ecosystem prepare for the future.

The uniquely explorative and execution-oriented mindset in Moomin management is a prerequisite for staying alert and competitive. Digitalizing, for example, has been a notably proactive endeavour, marked by Moomin curiosity and sense of adventure, something that has been discussed a lot among the employees, managers, and owners.

Looking ahead and being proactive is not only the prerogative of top management but it is encouraged for all. People are expected to take responsibility for their own actions. The spirit of love, equality, and courage means that everyone is expected to pull their weight. It is just a little bit easier to do this when you do not constantly feel someone breathing down your neck.

Rather than bossing them around, people are encouraged to manage themselves, like Maria Andersin did after her initial bafflement. People are, to use a provocative term, seduced to buy into the Moomin story and values and to live them voluntarily. This is not about working ridiculously long hours, but about engaging passionately with what Moomin is about. In this sense, people manage their own 'identities' or senses of self as Moomin employees.

There is a distinct risk in this approach. When people are left to manage themselves, they can choose not to do it – or to do it in a way that deviates from principles of generosity. Some want guidance and perhaps even someone to boss them around a bit, at least sometimes. Like in any system of people management, some will prevail and prosper at Moomin while others may be at a loss.

Keeping up resilience is also about managing differences in different societal and socio-cultural environments. However, we feel it is advisable to beware the popular concept of culture, especially national culture. This is because there is always the risk of essentializing it: you create an image of the world, and you start to believe that the world moves according to your image.

As far as people live them real, cultures are dynamic, and they change over time. History and conventions matter, but they do not, and cannot, explain everything in human behaviour and social interaction.

For example, Japan as a society is in many ways different today than it was decades ago. The Moomins have been enjoyed by generations of Japanese people since the 1960s, and their meaning has changed along with changes in society. Japanese consumers enjoy Moomins passionately, and they constantly expect new things to engage with.

Japanese aesthetics and innovations have proven invaluable for Moomin over the years. Moomin animations, Moomin Cafes, the Moomin theme park, and exclusive Moomin candy are examples of ideas generated in Japan.

Cultures are complex too. They do not lend themselves to simplistic understandings. There are always differences within cultures that make broad-brush explanations obsolete. In the UK, there seem to be some variations between different parts of the country in terms of what is appreciated as art and entertainment. What sells well in London or Brighton may not do so in Leeds or Newcastle, and vice versa.

Also, class-based differences in lifestyles and preferences for entertainment are perhaps a bit more prevalent in the UK than in some other countries. Moomins seem to appeal particularly to middle-class people, although there are plenty of exceptions to the rule. Finding receptive audiences and attracting new ones is a never-ending quest for Moomin.

Finally, cultures are relative. 'Finnish management' is a classic example. Research on Finnish–Swedish and Finnish–Russian multinational corporations demonstrates this. Straddling West and East, Finland has been influenced by its neighbours on both sides over the years.

While Finnish management is sometimes considered as harsh and authoritarian by Swedes, it has been seen as soft and overly democratic in Russia, as international business scholar Alexei Koveshnikov and his colleagues argue based on their studies of Finnish multinational corporations operating there (this was before Russia waged war on the Ukraine).

Cultural understandings are contingent on the comparisons made, then, and on the position of those who do the comparing. Often, they are developed and used for purposes of politicking in organizations. How Moomin Characters is seen to manage the brand and people is likely to vary according to context. The principles and practices that work in Finland must be adjusted to local conditions in societies across the world.

The Moomin story and values serve as a vantage point, but they may gain somewhat different meanings in different circumstances and cultural conditions. Perhaps employees in some contexts expect a bit of control and monitoring, for example, in the vein of traditional performance management. Emphasis on people managing themselves is something that cannot be embraced in the same way across the world.

At the same time, while Moomin management builds on some quintessentially Finnish and Nordic ideals such as equality and equal worth of people, associating Moomin management with Finnishness is a crude generalization. Few Finnish companies operate like Moomin does.

This is not to say that institutional contexts do not matter. They do because they set the scene for doing business. And habits and conventions are not irrelevant; they just play out in a multitude of ways. They must be understood and managed accordingly.

Differences within the Moomin ecosystem and across its strategic partners around the world reflect the make-up of the societies in question. Managing differences in Finland takes somewhat different forms from managing differences in the UK or Japan. Or even next door in Sweden.

Sensitivity to differences, cultural and other, is not only crucial for navigating in the increasingly complex global marketplace but a significant part of managing a resilient organization. Showing respect to people and their different ways of doing things is always important.

It seems to us that the Moomin ecosystem is culturally resilient at home and overseas. It breathes – meaning it offers a stimulating space for its people to interact – because it is based on a sense of purpose and togetherness.

Sometimes this plays out as tough management in support of Moomin employees when they are confronted with strategic partners not doing what has been agreed. We heard a story about an overseas partner breaching a contract and the Moomin employee overseeing the partnership being at a loss in dealing with the issue. Moomin top management intervened, threatening legal action, and the partner backed down to honour the agreement.

All the brave people and their humour

Sharing emotions is a big part of how Moomin Characters and the ecosystem function. The way organizational members are treated creates a space where all can feel and sense that they are respected and cared for. Generosity must be felt and sensed.

Positive emotions such as happiness and joy are expressed and shared at Moomin. Negative emotions, too, come into the open. Sadness and anger are expressed and shared. Sometimes the grief that is shared can seem overwhelming at first.

Marina Lindström feels deeply about Moomin, its values, and its people. Some time ago, she was diagnosed with cancer. After the initial shock, Marina decided that she wanted to continue working. "I wanted to work during the treatments so that I had something meaningful to do and think about. And I couldn't be more grateful for my workplace, how they have let me be sick and let me work all that time," Marina recalled all that she had been through before we interviewed her. "Working at Moomin kept me sane!"

Recalling her experiences, Marina shed a tear and continued: "Sorry, I wasn't supposed to cry but it's been a tough year, and this is so important ... that when something like this happens to you, the company doesn't abandon you." She went on:

> 'My colleagues here at Moomin bought bracelets that said, "Fuck cancer!" and gave them to everyone. When I joined them for a video meeting, everyone raised their hands to show it, and I got a photo of them with the text, "You can do it!" And all the cards I received in each phase ... the chemotherapy, the surgeries, and so on. I am just so grateful.'

How people who are broken are treated at Moomin caught our eye. By being broken, we refer broadly to vulnerability and to bad states and circumstances that people may find themselves in. Illness such as cancer is one example. However, people can be broken for other reasons, too, such as stress or burnout. Studying the Moomin ecosystem we witnessed how people were helped and supported when they were down.

We met people such as Marina Lindström who were very open about their problems. Many were articulate in verbalizing how they deal with being broken. They told us how Moomin helps and supports them in recovering from their challenges and problems. Others chose to keep a lid on things.

An actor in the Moomin ecosystem experienced burnout a few years ago. They were on a business trip abroad and just could not get out of bed one morning. The people around them expressed their caring and support, and the burnout victim could gradually come back to work, with reduced responsibilities at first, like Marina Lindström during her cancer treatments.

Top decision-makers in Moomin Characters have different backgrounds. They do not exactly have standard resumés for corporate bigwigs. Perhaps what they themselves have been through in life helps them to show empathy and care towards others.

With her experiences of fighting cancer, Marina Lindström reflected on Moomin management:

'It is a family business, of course, but I think it's more about the way the key people are. Sometimes when people get rich, they lose touch with how it is to live on a normal salary. Here, they still have a heart, feelings, and they know how normal people live.'

Sophia Jansson, Chairperson of the Moomin Characters Ltd board, was educated as a teacher and she taught Spanish language. Sophia spent many years abroad before returning to Finland to join the family firm in 1997. Her father Lars died some three years later, and a year after that Tove passed away. Suddenly, Sophia had to take charge of the family business.

For some time, Sophia felt lonely, and she feared that she was not able to preserve Tove's legacy. She then realized that she could only do her best and try to find the right people around her. While not being broken in the way that some others have been, through serious illness or burnout, Sophia can relate to their experiences.

Roleff Kråkström emphasizes the preventive side of things so that people would not be broken in the first place. "We systematically nip all clique mentality and bullying in the bud," Roleff stated firmly and went on to explain:

'I was bullied at school, and I know what it feels like when you are down. I also had a patch of rough times with my previous employer. I know how it feels to be beaten up at work, metaphorically speaking. I don't want others to feel what I have felt.'

Of course, some people are broken in private, and they are not comfortable with talking about it or making it public. We can only assume that they, too, benefit from the supportive atmosphere that by all accounts prevails at Moomin. It helps people to feel brave together.

How all the broken people are treated is the ultimate test for generosity and courage in the Moomin ecosystem. The courage to be vulnerable is the most important form of courage – and the most difficult. And so very Moomin.

★★★

While managing people at Moomin is characterized by love, equality, and courage, there is another side to the functioning of the organization that complicates things: humour. We witnessed what can only be described as an original sense of humour that is characteristic of the way people relate to each other at Moomin. Humour does not always seem to carry meanings of love, but humour and love can be connected nevertheless.

Marina Lindström told us how she enjoys the humour, joking, and laughing at Moomin. This is a big part of how she sees the Moomin organization and its people, and it was something that helped her through her tribulations. Marina has worked closely with Roleff Kråkström. "Rolle is a salesman who could sell his grandmother," Marina laughed. "But he has a big heart, which is the most important thing at the end of the day."

Shared humour can help create a sense of togetherness. To foster love, humour needs to come from the heart, and it cannot be nasty or vindictive. Love is lost when humour becomes subject to power plays and politicking.

With these caveats, it is clear that there would be no Moomin without humour. Tove Jansson's work exhibited a curious mix of humour and melancholy. Her humour did not deny sadness or grief. Often her humour was found between the lines, and it took the form of irony and parody. In its different forms, however, Tove's humour was always accepting, understanding, and compassionate. It showed the importance of equality and courage. It was positive and generous.

Humour liberates and it may well be related to experiences of happiness. Research suggests that positive humour – much like generosity – is associated with self-esteem, optimism, and satisfaction in life as well as with decreases in depression, anxiety, and stress. Positive humour would seem like a good way to help and support people who are broken.

The Moomin Group onboarding booklet is silent about humour, and unsurprisingly so. Humour is a delicate question, and its impact on how the organization functions is very difficult to pin down. Telling people to be humorous in a specific way would be absurd – and impossible.

Humour is also very difficult to analyse. When analysed it can become a serious matter. Writer E.B. White famously remarked that 'humor can be dissected, as a frog can, but the thing dies in the process and the innards are discouraging to any but the pure scientific mind'.

Managing people at Moomin is peppered with humour. It surfaces in relations and interaction among top decision-makers such as Sophia Jansson, Roleff Kråkström, Thomas Zambra, and James Zambra. They openly joke about each other in front of others. They help others to join in laughter when they manage by example.

However, we observed that there is also a sense of harshness at times in Moomin humour. Wild and witty humour can turn prickly. It can be interpreted in different ways, and sometimes it can lead to misunderstandings.

Humour is important because tensions and conflicts are a natural part of any community, and people need to be able to let off steam from time to time. At the workplace, humour acts as a safety valve sometimes when pressure mounts and people get tense.

Humour is to be found at Moomin when people interact with their bosses or among peers. It is crucial that humour does not get too personal and that no-one loses face in front of others. Managing with humour is delicate.

In everyday interaction involving many people, humour takes different guises. Spontaneous humour can lighten up a conversation over a cup of coffee, in a meeting, or at a workshop. We witnessed several instances where an appropriate humorous remark helped unlock a tense moment or take the discussion to a new level.

Monthly meetings that all employees are welcome to attend are an established management practice at Moomin Characters. Humour is very much present in these meetings. It reflects a sense of equality at Moomin, as Marina Lindström suggested. Everyone is allowed to be humorous, and everyone's humour is at least tolerated, if not always directly appreciated.

Staff meetings with everyone present offer a setting for shared humour and joking. In discussing facilities in the new fancy building where Moomin was going to move, one of the people present in the meeting asked: "And your jacuzzi, Roleff? Where will that be located?"

Amid a roar of laughter, Roleff said with a smile that "I am not an enthusiastic bather. I prefer showers." We witnessed many times how some people felt comfortable poking fun at Roleff in staff meetings, and how he kept the joke going.

It seemed to us that Moomin employees are dedicated to their jobs and enjoy each other's company. They work hard. Jokes about 'never having to go home' when discussing the new facilities in the staff meeting reflect a way of dealing with the fast pace and the stress, but also a way of mimicking dedication or even mocking the dedication that they have.

Marina Lindström laughed: "My child asked if someone was living at the office, and now I can say that we are all living there." With humour, Moomin employees can make sense together who they are and who they are not and move freely between the two.

Humour and courage are yet tricky bedfellows. We have been told multiple times by different people how new organizational members at Moomin go through a baptism of fire when they engage with humour that is at times quintessentially harsh. We have seen how this works out in practice. Some newcomers are on board relatively quickly, while for others Moomin humour takes longer to come to terms with.

Humour and courage, then, look somewhat different when viewed by people in different positions. In less formal occasions such as functions and parties, humour tends to blossom freely. It blends into the fabric of interaction and runs wild and free. There is a lot of laughing at Moomin parties.

So perhaps Moomin humour overall is like Little My, the tiny but fierce friend of the Moomin family. Little My is brave, but also fiery and often irritable. When others are being overly sentimental, she brings them quickly back to earth with her acute observations. While reckless at times, however, Little My is honest, loyal, and reliable. And she is always prepared for everything.

Humour is typically a contextual affair, and it is difficult to understand from outside the community where it blossoms. We witnessed some gallows humour at Moomin that would shock people not directly associated with the people involved.

You must know the people who are engaged in this kind of humour to be able to understand its nuances, intentions, and consequences. It is very much based on trust, like the humour Marina Lindström engaged in with her colleagues while fighting cancer.

At Moomin, humour functions in many ways. It is the property of both the establishment and the rebels. Pulling rank with humour is never advised. Challenging authority with humour, in contrast, can be advisable at times in an organization marked by equality. Jokes about Roleff Kråkström and 'his jacuzzi' blend into the natural flow of things at Moomin meetings. In this case, it contributed to the lively and productive discussion about the new company premises.

Humour heals, but it can also hurt. Humour is simultaneously the superpower and the Achilles heel in managing people at Moomin. In terms of generosity, it is always on the edge.

Managing people generously

In managing people, generosity takes a multitude of forms at Moomin. It helps make recruitment choices and it helps people grow in their work. Yet there are many challenges and risks involved in managing people generously.

Existing research shows how a sense of generosity is related to employee benefits and compensation. A study by business scholar Daniel M. Cable and colleagues, for example, indicates that organizations that extend generous benefits not only attract high-quality talent but also foster a culture of commitment and satisfaction.

Organization and management scholar Jeffrey Pfeffer highlighted that generosity can offset economic constraints. Pfeffer found that employees often reciprocate through increased loyalty, commitment, and effort, which in the long run can be economically beneficial for organizations characterized by generosity.

Yet there is also a potentially dark side to generosity. In social psychology, Matthew L. Stanley and his colleagues studied how employees with a reputation for giving are selectively targeted for exploitation. In other words, people seen as generous can be burdened with extra tasks that they are not rewarded for.

All ideas about generosity that we have shared in the previous chapters culminate in managing people generously. This is where push comes to shove. Generosity is ultimately a human experience. It can be found in encounters between people and in how they relate to each other when they go about doing what they do every day.

Generosity is also present in human encounters with non-humans. Extended to taking care of all living beings and the environment, like the Baltic Sea, generosity resonates with the urgent need to reverse the trend of humans destroying our shared planet. It is a way to do responsibility and sustainability in a world that is facing unprecedented ecological and social challenges.

Generosity is typically, in its human-centric and individualistic form, associated with giving. It is about giving people a chance and giving them the benefit of the doubt. It is about giving people the authority that goes with their responsibility – and giving them latitude and due credit for their ideas and work. Generosity is about making people feel important.

Generosity is about giving, yes, but it is much more than that. This book is about redefining generosity and, fundamentally, about how circumstances and conditions are created at Moomin that enable and give rise to acts of generosity. Rather than individuals, it is about shared practices and ways of doing things. Following philosopher Rosalyn Diprose, we see generosity as an openness to others that is critical to our existence, sociality, and social formation. In terms of managing people, we redefine generosity to be about ways to foster relations that generate different kinds of difference and their appreciation.

This is a key characteristic of the Moomin ecosystem and one that makes it generous. Openness to differences draws from Tove Jansson's ideals and it finds new forms in the endeavours the ecosystem is engaged in. Managing differences, then, is not only about appreciating and respecting each other. It is about openness for meaningful change over time.

Beyond individuals, generosity is fundamentally important for developing a resilient organization that, to use a human metaphor, breathes. It is based on showing people how and why they matter, but it is also about taking their needs and feelings seriously.

This is reflected in how the organization relates to its stakeholders, which is reflected back in the organization. Management scholar Muhammed Aftab Alam and his colleagues' study suggests that companies that are generous in giving support are more robust and resilient than those receiving generosity.

All the broken people at Moomin show how managing people generously is about dealing with positive as well as negative emotions, taking care of people when they are successful and when they are down, and showing deference to them.

It is about encouraging everyone to be generous – and about being generous even when not all are generous back. At Moomin, then, it is mostly about 'targeted generosity' or instances where the effects of generosity on given people or issues are known.

Can humour be generous then? This is where we see the boundaries of generosity at work. While humour can be a generator of generosity, we witnessed encounters between people at Moomin where humour was not received the way it was intended, and where humour seems to have hurt more than it healed, unintentionally, but nevertheless so.

In popular management thought, humour is subject to varying degrees of instrumentalism. Managers are encouraged to use different styles of humour to achieve organizational outcomes such as reducing stress, enhancing group cohesiveness, or fostering creativity. Humour is used to highlight discrepancies in logic and beliefs and to enable shifts in perspectives.

These assertions come with caution, as Alison Beard, executive editor of *Harvard Business Review*, reminds us, because humour is subjective and dependent on context. It must be used with extreme care. 'It's not whether or not you're funny, it's what kind of funny you are. Be honest and authentic', marketing and psychology scholar Peter McGraw and journalist Joel Warner conclude in their global search of what makes things funny.

While we did not see much care being taken (or rules and control) when embracing humour at Moomin, it did not seem to lead to irreparable damage. Humour can be dangerous, but we never witnessed anything like that at Moomin.

In her illuminative study of humour in an IT company, organization scholar Ursula Plesner reverted to how the dominant CEO displayed hegemonic masculinity while rejecting and mocking alternative expressions of being a man. A particular masculine ideal was forcefully displayed by the CEO in his constant performances of sexualized, sexist, and aggressive humour. Through these performances, which others were pressured to copy, the CEO exerted control over the organization and established a particularly toxic form of dominant masculinity, all in the name of humour, joking, and fun.

Figure 7.1: Friends forever

Source: © Moomin Characters™

Luckily, there is also a naturally positive side to humour. Humour is a useful vehicle of generosity because it enables juxtaposing otherwise incongruous or contradictory elements in organizations. In specific circumstances it can be a powerful way of expressing taboo feelings and impulses. Under the 'moral smokescreen' supplied by humour, organizations scholar Yiannis Gabriel and his colleagues suggest, people can express some of the ambiguities they feel.

Yet humour is never neutral. It can be both the prerogative of those in authority and an instrument for resistance. Humour can challenge management in highlighting inconsistencies and ambiguities in the organization, building on a shared recognition of contradiction or incoherence.

Ultimately, coming back to a more individualized idea of generosity, it is about learning to apologize when one has wronged and to forgive when one is wronged. As Martin Luther King Jr was quoted saying: 'That old law of an eye for an eye leaves everyone blind. The time is always right to do the right thing.'

No individual or organization is perfect. Aspiring to do good things and learning together is what matters most. It is impossible to be perfectly generous. Accepting this modestly, together, adds to generosity in the Moomin ecosystem. It can be a little rough around the edges, but that is alright.

8

Let's Party!

And now, dear readers, let's have a big party ... after all, we have deserved it.

We have come a long way, learning about Tove Jansson's ideas; exploring how the Moomin brand is protected and let to blossom; witnessing how strategic partnerships are formed and managed; exploring how strategy is done without a rigid plan; engaging with new technologies and entering digitalized and virtual worlds; and seeing how people are managed at Moomin with care and respect.

Tove Jansson, the creator of the Moomins, loved parties. This is how her friends and relatives remember her. Tove's love for parties can be seen in her biographically oriented texts and paintings. She described all kinds of bohemian celebrations in her artistic childhood home as well as in restaurants and park picnics across Helsinki and beyond.

Parties spice up life in the Moominvalley too. The moomin.com website told us that Moomins love to celebrate: 'Whether it's about a handbag that's been found, making it to safety, finding each other or the journey home, there's always a reason to party!' The principle is that everyone is welcome to celebrate. In moomin.com, Muskrat from Tove Jansson's book *Finn Family Moomintroll* was cited to set the tone and spirit for Moominous parties:

'You should have a lot of tables,' he said. 'Little tables and big ones – in unexpected places. Nobody wants to sit still in the same place at such a big party. There will be more fidgeting than usual, I'm afraid. And first you must offer them all the best things you have. Later on it's all the same what they get because they'll be enjoying themselves anyway. And don't disturb them with songs, and so on – let them make the program themselves.'

★★★

What does academic research have to say about Moomin parties then? Literary studies scholar Sirke Happonen (2012) has published a guide where over a hundred characters that have featured in Moomin books are depicted and analysed. She knows the Moomins and Moominvalley inside-out.

In one of her articles, Happonen (2014) studied parties in Tove Jansson's Moomin illustrations and texts. She argues that they can be understood as 'heterotopias'. This means that parties are 'places outside of all places, simultaneously both concrete and abstract'.

Sirke Happonen notes that Tove Jansson's Moomin stories regularly depict festive occasions and that almost every book includes a party scene. In the early Moomin books, Happonen argues, 'the party functions as a rather traditional children's literary scene: the moment of return and reunion as the characters come together, usually at the end of the adventure'. According to Happonen, 'The desire to celebrate sometimes even makes the characters forget the exciting journey they have been involved in'.

Happonen further argues that over time, as the Moomin books 'become more realistic and their landscape more Nordic … their parties no longer convey such absolute collective euphoria'. She yet concludes that 'the significance of a party is even more central because it is performed as part of a ritual, and because it often indicates a point of transition'. According to Happonen, the collective happiness depicted in earlier Moomin books becomes in later books 'represented as fragments of divided experience'.

When we let academics put their minds to it and analyse parties, it all becomes suddenly quite complicated. And, of course, not everyone in the Moomin books is fond of parties, especially parties of a more spontaneous nature. The Hemulens in their attentiveness to planning and order seem to despise the senseless ways in which others are enjoying themselves.

Perhaps inevitably, then, our projection of parties in the Moominvalley (in fiction) to make sense of the Moomin business ecosystem (in real life) is a limited one. But let's not have that spoil the fun.

In all their incarnations, parties are a good way to share emotions, celebrate together, and spread joy. Even the smallest of parties can help release us momentarily from the tribulations of everyday life. Unsurprisingly, social psychologists tell us that celebrating is a natural human tendency. It is good for us, plain and simple.

★★★

Generous parties are common practice in and around Moomin Characters Ltd, the company that is responsible for Moomin copyright supervision at the core of the business ecosystem. Conditions of the COVID-19 pandemic challenged this, and everyone was keen to get active with parties again.

In the Moomin values workshop we heard someone say with a sigh: "When a new employee comes into the company, at least their team should have a dinner and a small party. We have a party debt for those who joined during

Covid." We asked Sophia Jansson and Roleff Kråkström what a 'party debt' was, and Sophia told us: "We haven't had a party for a long time!" Roleff said:

'We have a very long tradition with our agents, partners and internally, to have these recurring parties in autumn and spring, where everyone is invited regardless of how long you have been with the company. A couple of years ago we took all employees to Japan to see the new theme park. Parties act as social glue in the onboarding process. So, we are ashamed and sad about the debt.'

Sometime later, Sophia added to the topic: "We have discussed a lot about the party debt. How we really miss being together."

However, parties are no quick fix – they must fit the normal flow of things in the organization. Trust is a precondition for fun initiatives to be considered appropriate by employees, psychology scholars Katerina Georganta and Anthony Montgomery remind us. Shared fun can then help build further trust and engagement. According to Georganta and Montgomery, when the company seeks to organize fun, cynicism can arise if employees see a mismatch between carefully orchestrated events and their everyday austere existence in the organization.

This is not the case at Moomin. Our ethnographic study led us to see how parties are a fundamentally important part of the Moomin philosophy and how they help narrate the shared Moomin story.

Although those involved may not necessarily see it as such, we understand parties to be an important management practice at Moomin. Celebrating and having fun together is fantastic for its own sake, but it also serves as a means of retaining the sense of common purpose and togetherness that is so vital to generosity at Moomin. Apart from all other practices covered in this book, parties offer a unique setting where the Moomin story can be lived real: outside the workplace (at least in spirit) but still attached to it.

Different kinds of parties are held at Moomin, everything from big celebrations to small social gatherings. When dressing up for the former, people can set aside their everyday worries and experience a heightened sense of social unity and togetherness. At best, big celebrations help to release tension and to garner energy.

The choreography of a party can be meticulously planned, although this does not really seem to be the case at Moomin. Choosing the location and venue is crucial for setting the right tone in the celebration. Who to invite and how to set up the programme – there are multiple ways to put structure around a party and to frame it so that its intended purpose can be fulfilled.

At the same time, it is advisable, as we are told by Muskrat, to let the guests 'make the program themselves'. This is yet another eternal management balancing act. It is about balancing between structuring parties and letting them flow – control and freedom. At Moomin, the latter tends to overcome the former.

Some parties at Moomin resemble a carnival. Well, without the over-indulgence. They involve the whole community and mark an important occasion. Moomin parties do not, however, represent a ritual where social roles are reversed and norms about desired behaviour get suspended, something that is central to the Christian carnival tradition. Kings do not become beggars and beggars do not become kings for a day. Perhaps we can just call Moomin parties carnivalesque?

Or, then again, maybe not. In her analysis of parties in Tove Jansson's Moomin books, Sirke Happonen (2014) takes distance to this idea. Moomin books do not reflect carnivalesque features of turning things upside down. Moominous parties and celebrations are something unique and special, but they are not really anarchist.

Big celebrations at Moomin, in real life, are held to mark occasions such as Christmas, New Year's Eve, or birthdays. The Jansson family is symbolically extended. Those present are embraced and taken in to share precious moments together. Sometimes extended family members offer surprises for all.

★★★

Humour is an inescapable part of Moomin parties. Sometime ago, a Christmas party was held as a fancy dress with the special theme 'Paris'. While most – including Sophia Jansson who dressed as a dancing girl at the Moulin Rouge – interpreted the theme to refer to the glorious capital city of France, the City of Lights, someone came as the spitting image of Paris Hilton, the American celebrity woman.

Well, as much the spitting image of Paris H that a tall and muscular man can be. The tight dress and accessories being the opposite of how he may present in the office, the others responded with humour and surprise. One recent young recruit to the Moomin ecosystem, however, was caught staring at 'Paris H' with a dropped jaw and muttering that "I thought this was about Paris in France".

A touch of the carnivalesque, perhaps? For some, it takes a while to get the hang of Moomin humour. And some may think the performance as 'Paris H' was vulgar and in poor taste. It was different, that's for sure.

It is interesting to note that 'Paris H' had not been with the organization for long and that it was only his second Moomin party. That he understood the theme, and then decided to turn it upside down with an intentional misunderstanding, was a bold and witty move. As such, it was appreciated by many.

While the Paris party turned into something of a spectacle, smaller social gatherings are also held at Moomin. In times of the COVID-19 pandemic, parties were held that were more low-key than wished and reluctantly organized online. These were parties that everyone would have liked to be bigger, but turned out smaller, due to circumstances. They were about savouring moments together nevertheless. They were about welcoming someone to the team or saying farewell.

All kinds of parties have a meaning. When good things happen to us, we want to share the experience with others. Spreading happiness is important. Also, when bad things happen, sharing helps. Laughing it out together may be the only solution available to us. We party and we move on.

How about party politics, then? Not political party politics but using celebrations to bolster one's own position and prestige? There is perhaps no way of avoiding that; for some people parties are first and foremost a way to show off and draw attention to themselves. Curiously enough, we have seen very little of this at Moomin. The 'no heroes' principle seems to stretch to parties too.

In the end, parties are about storytelling. They are significant for creating shared experiences and memories – and adding nuances to the shared Moomin story.

★★★

Some of the 'party debt' at Moomin could finally be paid back when Sophia Jansson's birthday party was held. A lot of people attended and the atmosphere was festive and distinctly warm. There was joy and hope in the air, despite all the terrible things happening across the world.

A lot of family and friends came to celebrate Sophia. These included employees of Moomin Group and several more from Rights & Brands. The heads of many companies that cooperate with Moomin attended. And a few past partners who are not so involved in the business anymore.

Although many who attended the party were wealthy and others famous, or both, from the moment the guests checked their coats, it felt special. It felt that here it would be okay to let one's social guard down and not face judgement or criticism. The party, like Moomin at large, was somehow a safe place. Not entirely, perhaps, but more so than many other big social gatherings.

Some Moomin employees performed a scene between Moomintroll and Snorkmaiden that was humorous and emotional, showing how they see Sophia and her unique relationship with the Moomin. The scene was about kindness and sociability, and courage too.

Roleff's speech to Sophia, his wife, was special. He reflected on global conflicts and crises over the past decades, and how totalitarian dictators move against free press, authors, and the freedom to think for oneself. Roleff emphasized literature as a medium that is particularly dangerous for totalitarianism. Being able to read, and reading widely, is in this sense a type of rebellion – not to speak of writing. All those things that are dear to Moomin, and to Sophia, offer a counterweight to all the grimness in the world.

Sophia's party was held in a large hall and the acoustics turned out to be rather poor. Despite the more than a hundred people attending there were odd pockets of isolation. No-one could hear anyone other than the people sat nearby. If people around you were engaged in the other direction, you could have a private, one-on-one discussion with someone else.

The curious whispering in the ear, laughing or frowning, and the closeness seemed incongruous in the context of the greater throng of people present. Yet it was only possible because of the throng and the noise. The party was at the same time grand and intimate.

And there was a lot dancing. Sophia loves dancing.

As dinner was ending, all guests were invited to step out onto the terrace and balcony. Across the small bay, fireworks were set off. There was a strong reaction, cheering and 'oo'-ing and 'aah'-ing at the rainbow of colours in the sky.

Figure 8.1: Let's party!

Source: © Moomin Characters™

A party like this says that life is to be lived and that friends and family are to be celebrated. Love, equality, and courage, the Moomin values, and tolerance, of course, are more important than ever. Generosity.

Then the guests went back in and danced some more.

★★★

Throughout this book we have stressed the need to redefine generosity in managing businesses and organizations in the contemporary global economy. Partying the Moomin way brings one final piece to the puzzle. Parties offer opportunities to be generous, spread generosity, and feel and sense generosity. There is also a strong symbolic element to generosity at parties.

Moomin parties are about sharing and giving. They are about openness to differences. When everyone is invited, and everyone is welcomed for who they are, a grounding for generosity is created.

While most of our examples throughout this book are about everyday generosity – be it in relation to consumers, partners, or employees – the magical moments people share at parties add to the mix. They give an opportunity to celebrate generosity together. Dance. Enjoy the fireworks. And dance again.

After all, in a great party, we can forget our worries for a little while. Then the quest continues to make the world a better place for all – the Moomin way.

References

Abrahamson, Eric (2004) *Change without pain: How managers can overcome initiative overload, organizational chaos, and employee burnout*. Boston, MA: Harvard Business School Press.

Alam, Muhammed Aftab, Rooney, David, Lundmark, Erik and Taylor, Murray (2023) The ethics of sharing: Does generosity erode the competitive advantage of an ecosystem firm? *Journal of Business Ethics* 187: 821–39.

Alvesson, Mats (2022) *The triumph of emptiness: Consumption, higher education, and work organization* (2nd edn). Oxford: Oxford University Press.

Alvesson, Mats and Sveningsson, Stefan (2003) Managers doing leadership: The extra-ordinarization of the mundane. *Human Relations* 56(12): 1435–59.

Baldauf, Heike, Develotte, Christine and Ollagnier-Beldame, Magali (2017) The effects of social media on the dynamics of identity: Discourse, interaction, and digital traces. *Alsic* 20: 1–19.

Barwise, Patrick and Meehan, Sean (2010) The one thing you must get right when building a brand. *Harvard Business Review*, December: 80–4.

Beard, Alison (2014) Leading with humor. *Harvard Business Review*, May: 130–1.

Belfiore, Eleonora (2020) Whose cultural value? Representation, power and creative industries. *International Journal of Cultural Policy* 26(3): 383–97.

Bell, Emma and Leonard, Pauline (2018) Digital organizational storytelling on YouTube: Constructing plausibility through network protocols of amateurism, affinity, and authenticity. *Journal of Management Inquiry* 27: 330–51.

Berry, Leonard L. (2007) The best companies are generous companies. *Business Horizons* 50(4): 263–9.

Boje, David M. (1995) Stories of the storytelling organization: A postmodern analysis of Disney as 'Tamara Land'. *Academy of Management Journal* 38: 997–1035.

Brunila, Mikael, Saarinen, Vilja and Sandell, Valter (2023) *Kuulumme toisillemme – kirjeitä ja kirjoituksia ystävyyden politiikasta* [We belong to each other – letters and writings on the politics of friendship]. Helsinki: Khaos Publishing.

Cable, Daniel M., Gino, Francesca and Staats, Bradley R. (2013) Breaking them in or eliciting their best? Reframing socialization around newcomers' authentic self-expression. *Administrative Science Quarterly* 58(1): 1–36.

Cameron, Kim S., Dutton, Jane E. and Quinn, Robert E. (eds) (2003) *Positive organizational scholarship: Foundations of a new discipline.* San Francisco, CA: Berrett-Koehler Publishers.

Chandler, Alfred D. (1962) *Strategy and structure. Chapters in the history of the industrial enterprise.* Cambridge, MA: The MIT Press.

Chia, Robert and Holt, Robin (2010) *Strategy without design: The silent efficacy of indirect action.* Cambridge: Cambridge University Press.

Clarke, Arthur C. (1967) *Profiles of the future: An inquiry into the limits of the possible.* New York: Bantam Books.

Climate Leadership Coalition (2022) *Nordic CEOs' view of raised climate ambitions in the Nordic countries: An Interview study among leading businesses in the Nordics.* Haga Initiative (Sweden), Skift Business Climate Leaders (Norway) and Climate Leadership Coalition (Finland). Available from: https://clc.fi/wp-content/uploads/2022/01/Report-Nordic-CEOs-view-of-raised-climate-ambitions3.pdf [Accessed 6 June 2023].

Diprose, Rosalyn (2002) *Corporeal generosity: On giving with Nietzsche, Merleau-Ponty, and Levinas.* Albany, NY: Suny Press.

Dunn, Elizabeth W., Aknin, Lara B. and Norton, Michael I. (2008) Spending money on others promotes happiness. *Science* 319(5870): 1687–8.

Einola, Katja, Khoreva, Violetta and Tienari, Janne (2023) A colleague named Max: A critical inquiry into affects when an anthropomorphised AI (ro)bot enters the workplace. *Human Relations*, OnlineFirst.

Faraj, Samer and Pachidi, Stella (2021) Beyond Uberization: The co-constitution of technology and organizing. *Organization Theory* 2(1): 1–14.

Fleming, Peter (2019) Robots and organization studies: Why robots might not want to steal your job. *Organization Studies* 40(1): 23–38.

Fleming, Peter and Sturdy, Andrew (2009) 'Just be yourself!': Towards neo-normative control in organisations? *Employee Relations* 31(6): 569–83.

Freeman, R. Edward, Parmar, Bidhan L. and Martin, Kirsten (2020) *The power of and: Responsible business without trade-offs.* New York, NY: Columbia University Press.

Gabriel, Yiannis, Fineman, Stephen and Sims, David (2000) *Organizing and organizations.* London: Sage.

Garcia, Claudio (2022) The power of generosity in ecosystems. *Strategy+ Business.* Available from: [https://www.strategy-business.com/article/The-power-of-generosity-in-ecosystems [Accessed 28 June 2023].

Geng, Ruoqi, Lam, Hugo K.S. and Stevenson, Mark (2022) Addressing modern slavery in supply chains: An awareness-motivation-capability perspective. *International Journal of Operations & Production Management* 42(3): 331–56.

Georganta, Katerina and Montgomery, Anthony (2022) Workplace fun is not enough: The role of work engagement and trust. *Cogent Psychology* 9(1).

Gibson, James J. (1979) *The ecological approach to visual perception.* Boulder, CO: Harper & Collins.

Grant, Robert M. (2010) *Contemporary strategy analysis* (8th edn). Chichester, UK: John Wiley & Sons.

Guillén, Mauro F. and García-Canal, Esteban (2012) Execution as strategy. *Harvard Business Review*, October: 103–7.

Hamari, Juho (2017) Do badges increase user activity? A field experiment on effects of gamification. *Computers in Human Behavior* 71: 469–78.

Hamel, Gary and Välikangas, Liisa (2003) The quest for resilience. *Harvard Business Review*, September: 52–63.

Happonen, Sirke (2012) *Muumiopas: Tove ja Lars Janssonin muumiteosten alkuperäishahmot* [Moomin guide: Original figures in Tove and Lars Jansson's works on Moomin]. Helsinki: SKS.

Happonen, Sirke (2014) Parties as heterotopias in Tove Jansson's Moomin illustrations and texts. *Lion and the Unicorn – A Critical Journal of Children's Literature* 38: 182–99.

Heidrick & Struggles (2021) *Board Monitor Europe 2021.* Available from: https://www.heidrick.com/en/insights/boards-governance/board-monitor-europe-2021 [Accessed 6 June 2023].

Hjorth, Daniel and Holt, Robin (2016). It's entrepreneurship, not enterprise: Ai Weiwei as entrepreneur. *Journal of Business Venturing Insights* 5: 50–4.

Holt, Douglas B. (2004) *How brands become icons: The principles of cultural branding.* Boston, MA: Harvard Business School Press.

hooks, bell (2000) *All about love: New visions.* New York: Harper Collins.

Inagaki, Tristen K. and Ross, Lauren P. (2018) Neural correlates of giving social support: Differences between giving targeted versus untargeted support. *Psychosomatic Medicine: Journal of Biobehavioral Medicine* 80(8): 724–32.

Iser, Wolfgang (1993) *The fictive and the imaginary: Charting literary anthropology.* Baltimore, MA: Johns Hopkins University Press.

Kärreman, Dan and Rylander, Anna (2008) Managing meaning through branding: The case of a consulting firm. *Organization Studies* 29(1): 103–25.

Khurana, Rakesh (2002) The curse of the superstar CEO. *Harvard Business Review*, September: 60–6.

Klisanin, Dana (2011) Is the internet giving rise to new forms of altruism? *Media Psychology Review* 3(1). Available from: https://mprcenter.org/review/internetdigitalaltruism/ [Accessed 6 June 2023].

Kornberger, Martin (2010) *Brand society: How brands transform management and lifestyle.* Cambridge: Cambridge University Press.

Kornberger, Martin (2013) Disciplining the future: On studying the politics of strategy. *Scandinavian Journal of Management* 29: 104–7.

Koveshnikov, Alexei, Vaara, Eero and Ehrnrooth, Mats (2016) Stereotype-based managerial identity work in multinational corporations. *Organization Studies* 37: 1353–79.

Laajarinne, Jukka (2009) *Muumit ja olemisen arvoitus* [Moomins and the mystery of being]. Jyväskylä: Atena.

Landry, Lauren (2019) Tips for scaling your business. *Harvard Business School Online Business Insights.* 7 March 2019. [online] Available from: https://onl ine.hbs.edu/blog/post/how-to-scale-a-business [Accessed 6 June 2023].

Lindebaum, Dirk, Vesa, Mikko and den Hond, Frank (2020) Insights from 'The Machine Stops' to better understand rational assumptions in algorithmic decision-making and its implications for organizations. *Academy of Management Review* 45: 247–63.

Louvrier, Jonna (2013) *Diversity, difference and diversity management: A contextual and interview study of managers and ethnic minority employees in Finland and France.* Economics and Society Vol 259. Helsinki: Hanken School of Economics.

Mantere, Saku and Vaara, Eero (2008) On the problem of participation in strategy: A critical discursive perspective. *Organization Science* 19: 341–58.

March, James G. (1991) Exploration and exploitation in organizational learning. *Organization Science* 2: 71–87.

Martinuzzi, Bruna (2009) *The leader as a Mensch: Become the kind of person others want to follow.* San Francisco, CA: Six Seconds Emotional Intelligence Press.

Matthiessen, Christian M.I.M. (2022) The Moomin family: An elastic permeable multi-dimensional construct in semiotic and social space. In A. Jesús Moya-Guijarro and Eija Ventola (eds) *A multimodal approach to challenging gender stereotypes in children's picture books.* New York: Routledge, pp 268–305.

Mauborgne, Renée and Kim, W. Chan (2004) *Blue ocean strategy: How to create uncontested market space and make the competition irrelevant.* Boston, MA: Harvard Business School Publishing.

McAfee, Andrew and Brynjolfsson, Erik (2012) Big Data: The management revolution. *Harvard Business Review,* October: 59–68.

McGrath, Paul, McCarthy, Lucy, Marshall, Donna and Rehme, Jakob (2021) Tools and technologies of transparency in sustainable global supply chains. *California Management Review* 64(1): 67–89.

McGraw, Peter and Warner, Joel (2014) *The humor code: A global search for what makes things funny.* New York: Simon & Schuster.

Mielly, Michelle, Islam, Gazi and Gosen, Dora (2023) Better sorry than safe: Emotional discourses and neo-normative control in a workplace safety council. *Organization Studies* 44(6): 889–917.

Mintzberg, Henry (1987) The strategy concept I: Five Ps for strategy. *California Management Review* 30(1): 11–24.

Mintzberg, Henry (1994) *The rise and fall of strategic planning. Reconceiving roles for planning, plans, planners.* New York: Free Press.

Moore, James F. (1996) *The death of competition: Leadership and strategy in the age of business ecosystems.* New York: Harper Business

Mumby, Dennis K. (2016) Organizing beyond organization: Branding, discourse, and communicative capitalism. *Organization* 23: 884–907.

Nonaka, Ikujiro and Takeuchi, Hirotaka (2011) The big idea: The wise leader. *Harvard Business Review*, May.

O'Neil, Cathy (2016) *Weapons of math destruction. How Big Data increases inequality and threatens democracy.* Largo, MA: Crown Books.

Orwell, George (1945) *Animal farm: A fairy story.* London: Secker & Warburg.

Park, Soyoung, Kahnt, Thorsten, Dogan, Azade, Strang, Sabrina, Fehr, Ernst and Tobler, Philippe N. (2017) A neural link between generosity and happiness. *Nature Communications* 8, article 15964.

Pfeffer, Jeffrey (2010) Building sustainable organizations: The human factor. *Academy of Management Perspectives* 24(1): 34–45.

Plesner, Ursula (2015) 'Take it like a man!': Performing hegemonic masculinity through organizational humour. *Ephemera* 15(3): 537–59.

Porter, Michael E. (1980) *Competitive strategy: Techniques for analyzing industries and competitors.* New York: Free Press.

Pulkkis, Nina and Vähäkylä, Liisa (2017) *Muumeista miljoonabisnes* [Making Moomin into a business of millions]. Helsinki: Siltala.

Ricoeur, Paul (1981) *Hermeneutics and the human sciences: Essays on language, action and interpretation.* Cambridge: Cambridge University Press.

Södergren, Jonatan (2021) Brand authenticity: 25 Years of research. *International Journal of Consumer Studies* 45(4): 645–663.

Stanley, Matthew L., Neck, Christopher P. and Neck, Christopher B. (2023) The dark side of generosity: Employees with a reputation for giving are selectively targeted for exploitation. *Journal of Experimental Social Psychology* 108: 104503.

Such, Elizabeth, Jaipaul, Ravi and Salway, Sarah (2020) Modern slavery in the UK: How should the health sector be responding? *Journal of Public Health* 42(1): 216–20.

Toubiana, Madeline and Zietsma, Charlene (2017) The message is on the wall? Emotions, social media and the dynamics of institutional complexity. *Academy of Management Journal* 60(3): 922–53.

Ulrich, Dave, Younger, Jon, Brockback, Wayne and Ulrich, Mike (2012) *HR from the outside in: Six competences for the future of human resources.* New York: McGraw Hill.

Vesa, Mikko and Tienari, Janne (2022) Artificial intelligence and rationalized unaccountability: Ideology of the elites? *Organization* 29(6): 1133–45.

Von Krogh, Georg (2018) Artificial intelligence in organizations: New opportunities for phenomenon-based theorizing. *Academy of Management Discoveries* 4(4): 404–9.

Wallin, Mark Rowell (2006) Myths, monsters and markets: Ethos, identification, and the video game adaptations of the Lord of the Rings. *Game Studies* 7(1).

Westin, Boel (2014) *Tove Jansson: Life, art, words: The authorised biography*. London: Sort of Books.

Whittington, Richard (2006) Completing the practice turn in strategy research. *Organization Studies* 27: 613–34.

Zanoni, Patrizia, Janssens, Maddy, Benschop, Yvonne and Nkomo, Stella M. (2010) Unpacking diversity, grasping inequality: Rethinking difference through critical perspectives. *Organization* 17: 9–29.

Media materials on Moomin

Allardice, Lisa (2019) 'It's a religion': How the world went mad for Moomins. *The Guardian*, [online] 6 April. Available from: https://www.theguardian.com/books/2019/apr/06/it-is-a-religion-how-the-world-went-mad-for-moomins [Accessed 29 January 2024].

Bosworth, Mark (2014) Tove Jansson: Love, war and the Moomins. *BBC News Magazine*, [online] 13 March. Available from: https://www.bbc.com/news/magazine-26529309 [Accessed 29 January 2024].

Clapp, Susannah (2021) How Tove Jansson's love of nature shaped the world of the Moomins. *The Observer*, [online] 5 June. Available from: https://www.theguardian.com/books/2021/jun/05/tove-jansson-moomins-woman-fell-in-love-with-an-island-summer-book [Accessed 29 January 2024].

Clark, Benjamin (2019) Moomin: The art and the story: The Moomins go to Japan. *The Comics Journal*, [online] 10 December. Available from: https://www.tcj.com/moomin-the-art-and-the-story-the-moomins-go-to-japan/ [Accessed 29 January 2024].

Doi, Shimpei (2021) DHC asked not to use Moomin characters after outrage online. *The Asahi Shimbun*, [online] 25 August. Available from: https://www.asahi.com/ajw/articles/14425592 [Accessed 29 January 2024].

Flood, Alison (2014) Tove Jansson should have won Nobel prize, says Philip Pullman. *The Guardian*, [online] 2 June. Available from: https://www.theguardian.com/books/2014/jun/02/tove-jansson-nobel-prize-philip-pullman [Accessed 29 January 2024].

Golby, Joel (2019) Why are Rosamund Pike and Kate Winslet stuck in the CGI Moominvalley? *The Guardian*, [online] 13 April. Available from: https://www.theguardian.com/tv-and-radio/2019/apr/13/moominvalley-sky-tv-rosamund-pike-kate-winslet [Accessed 29 January 2024].

Heti, Sheila (2020) Inside Tove Jansson's private universe. *The New Yorker*, [online] 30 March. Available from: https://www.newyorker.com/magazine/2020/04/06/inside-tove-janssons-private-universe [Accessed 29 January 2024].

Koskinen, Anu Leena (2018) Muumivillitys täytti sosiaalisen median vitsimukeilla: 'Muumiomuki 3200 euroa, jonoon järjesty!' [Moomin craze filled social media with humorous mugs: 'Moomin mug 3,200 euros – get in line!'] *Yle.fi*, [online] 10 August. Available from: https://yle.fi/a/3-10346316#:~:text=Tuomas%20Pakkanen%20esitteli%20Muumiomukin%2C%20jossa,h%C3%A4n%20kirjoittaa%20Twitteriss%C3%A4. [Accessed 29 January 2024].

License Global (2021) King Features expands Moomin's US presence, [online] 12 November. Available from: https://www.licenseglobal.com/fashion/king-features-expands-moomins-us-presence [Accessed 29 January 2024].

Luckel, Madeleine (2018) Moomins are Finland's favorite cartoon figures – Here's where to see them in Helsinki. *Vogue*, [online] 23 May. Available from: https://www.vogue.com/article/moomins-travel-helsinki-finland [Accessed 29 January 2024].

Lynn, Hyung-Gu (2016) Moomins ascendant in Asia: Interview with Moomin Characters Ltd. Managing Director Roleff Kråkström. *Asia Pacific Memo*, The University of British Columbia, [online] 22 March. Available from: https://apm.iar.ubc.ca/moomins-ascendant-in-asia/ [Accessed 29 January 2024].

Marten, Peter (2010) Moomin Characters Ltd keeps a national treasure in the family. *Finland.fi*, [online] April. Available from: https://finland.fi/business-innovation/moomin-characters-ltd-keeps-a-national-treasure-in-the-family/#:~:text=The%20Moomins%20are%20close%20to,Moomintroll%20and%20the%20Snork%20maiden [Accessed 29 January 2024].

Music Business Worldwide (2018) Sony Music inks deal to soundtrack new TV series based on classic Moomin stories, [online] 11 September. Available from: https://www.musicbusinessworldwide.com/sony-music-inks-deal-to-soundtrack-new-tv-series-based-on-classic-moomin-stories/ [Accessed 29 January 2024].

Muurinen, Anna (2015) Nuuskamuikkunen on japanilaismiesten idoli [Snufkin is the idol of Japanese men]. *Seura*, [online] 26 February. Available from: https://seura.fi/asiat/ajankohtaista/miksi-suomalaiset-ja-japanilaiset-tykkaavat-muumeista-saunasta-ja-karaokesta/ [Accessed 29 January 2024].

Raj Joshi, Abhaya and von Kügelgen, Michaela (2020) How the Moomins made their way into the hearts of Nepalis. *The Kathmandu Post*, [online] 3 December. Available from: https://kathmandupost.com/art-culture/2020/12/03/how-the-moomins-made-their-way-into-the-hearts-of-nepalis [Accessed 29 January 2024].

Räsänen, Piritta (2021) Twitterissä julkaistut kuvat vanhasta työstä 'laivamuumina' vaadittiin poistamaan – Moomin Characters: inhimillinen väärinkäsitys [Ordered to delete old pictures in Twitter on working as 'boat Moomin' – Moomin Characters: Human misunderstanding]. *Hs.fi*, [online] 5 May. Available from: https://www.hs.fi/nyt/art-2000007960196.html [Accessed 29 January 2024].

Singapore Comix (2017) Munching with the Moomins: Interview with Roleff Krakstrom, Managing Director of Moomin Characters Limited. [blog] 29 September. Available from: https://singaporecomix.blogspot. com/2017/09/munching-with-moomins-interview-with.html [Accessed 29 January 2024].

Terranova, Erica (2021) My SEO Journey: Erica Terranova from moomin. com – Growing in authority on a strong brand integrity. *Seobuddy.com*, [blog] 24 May. Available from: https://seobuddy.com/blog/my-seo-jour ney-moomin/ [Accessed 29 January 2024].

Tuomasjukka, Tuukka (2020) Muumit vedettiin mukaan Puolan aborttitaisteluun – Moomin Characters tuomitsi kiistellyn muutoksen puolustamisen 'pikkumuumeilla' [Moomin dragged into Polish abortion battle – Moomin Characters condemned defending the disputed change with 'little Moomin']. *Suomen Kuvalehti*, [online] 28 October. Available from: https://suomenkuvalehti.fi/ulkomaat/muumit-vedettiin-mukaan-puolan-aborttitaisteluun-moomin-characters-tuomitsi-kiistellyn-muutok sen-puolustamisen-pikkumuumeilla/ [Accessed 29 January 2024].

Index

References to figures appear in *italic* type.